GRANTS, LOANS, AND LOCAL CURRENCIES

Paper $1.50   Library edition in cloth $2.50

ROBERT E. ASHER

Grants, Loans, and Local Currencies

Their Role in Foreign Aid

THE BROOKINGS INSTITUTION • WASHINGTON, D. C.

© 1961 BY

THE BROOKINGS INSTITUTION

Published May 1961

Second Printing March 1962

Third Printing October 1966

Library of Congress Catalog Card Number 61-13988

THE BROOKINGS INSTITUTION is an independent organization engaged in research and education in the social sciences. Its principal purposes are to aid in the development of sound public policies and to provide advanced training for students in the social sciences.

The Institution was founded December 8, 1927, as a consolidation of three antecedent organizations: the Institute for Government Research, 1916; the Institute of Economics, 1922; and the Robert Brookings Graduate School of Economics and Government, 1924.

The general administration of the Institution is the responsibility of a self-perpetuating Board of Trustees. In addition to this general responsibility the By-Laws provide that, "It is the function of the Trustees to make possible the conduct of scientific research and publication, under the most favorable conditions, and to safeguard the independence of the research staff in the pursuit of their studies and in the publication of the results of such studies. It is not a part of their function to determine, control, or influence the conduct of particular investigations or the conclusions reached." The immediate direction of the policies, program, and staff of the Institution is vested in the President, who is assisted by an advisory council, chosen from the professional staff of the Institution.

In publishing a study, the Institution presents it as a competent treatment of a subject worthy of public consideration. The interpretations and conclusions in such publications are those of the author or authors and do not necessarily reflect the views of other members of the Brookings staff or of the administrative officers of the Institution.

BOARD OF TRUSTEES

WILLIAM R. BIGGS, *Chairman*
ROBERT BROOKINGS SMITH, *Vice Chairman*
DANIEL W. BELL, *Chairman, Executive Committee*

Arthur Stanton Adams
Dillon Anderson
Elliott V. Bell
Robert D. Calkins
Leonard Carmichael
Thomas H. Carroll
Colgate W. Darden, Jr.
Marion B. Folsom
William C. Foster
Huntington Gilchrist

Huntington Harris
John E. Lockwood
Morehead Patterson
Sydney Stein, Jr.
Gilbert F. White
Donald B. Woodward

Honorary Trustees

Mrs. Robert S. Brookings
John Lee Pratt

HAROLD G. MOULTON, *President Emeritus*
ROBERT D. CALKINS, *President*
ROBERT W. HARTLEY, *Vice President*
GEORGE A. GRAHAM, *Director of Governmental Studies*
H. FIELD HAVILAND, JR., *Director of Foreign Policy Studies*
JAMES M. MITCHELL, *Director of Conference Program on Public Affairs*
JOSEPH A. PECHMAN, *Executive Director, Studies of Government Finance*
RALPH J. WATKINS, *Director of Economic Studies*

Foreword

THIS BOOKLET on grants, loans, and local currencies attempts to shed light on some important, controversial, and ill-understood aspects of foreign aid. It deals with the theory and practice of granting, lending, and selling as they have evolved under bilateral and multilateral assistance programs during the turbulent years since the close of World War II. Its aim is the identification of issues and alternatives for the interested citizen rather than full-scale analysis for the benefit of specialists.

The present study should not be regarded as an isolated effort on the part of the Brookings Institution. Our concern with the administration and operation of foreign aid programs is of long standing. It antedates the Marshall Plan, includes both administrative and substantive aspects of aid programs, and embraces multilateral as well as bilateral undertakings. In January 1948, at the request of the late Senator Arthur H. Vandenberg, then Chairman of the Senate Committee on Foreign Relations, the Institution prepared a *Report on Administration of United States Aid for a European Recovery Program*. In 1951, pursuant to a request from the Bureau of the Budget, the Institution reported on the *Administration of Foreign Affairs and Overseas Operations,* with particular reference to the administration of economic and military assistance. In 1957, a study entitled *Administrative Aspects of United States Foreign Assistance Programs* was prepared at the request of the Special Senate Committee to Study the Foreign Aid Program. *The Formulation and Administration of United States Foreign Policy*, a report for the Committee on Foreign Relations of the United States Senate, printed in January 1960, includes more recent information on administrative aspects of aid programs.

In addition to these administrative studies, the Institution, on its own initiative, has analyzed substantive features of aid programs.

In 1951, Brookings published *Current Issues in Foreign Economic Assistance,* an interim report on a comprehensive analysis of American experience with foreign assistance during World War II and the early postwar years. The results of the study were incorporated in the volume *American Foreign Assistance,* by William Adams Brown and Redvers Opie, published in 1953. Other relevant Brookings publications include *United States Foreign Policy, 1945-1955,* by William Reitzel, Morton A. Kaplan, and Constance G. Coblenz (1956), *The United Nations and Promotion of the General Welfare,* by Robert E. Asher, Walter M. Kotschnig, and others (1957), *The Foreign Aid Expenditures of the United States,* by Robert E. Asher (Brookings Reprint No. 21, 1958), and *Foreign Aid and the Policy Process: 1957,* by H. Field Haviland, Jr. (Brookings Reprint No. 30, 1958). Additional studies are under way.

The author of the present booklet, Robert E. Asher, has been a member of the senior staff of the Brookings Institution since 1954, with a leave of absence during 1958-59 to serve with the Food and Agriculture Organization of the United Nations as head of an international team surveying the development potentialities of Morocco and Tunisia. Before coming to Brookings, he was for three years a Special Assistant to the Assistant Secretary of State for Economic Affairs and served for a total of nearly 20 years in the Federal Government.

The author and the Institution acknowledge with gratitude the thoughtful comments and constructive suggestions of the Advisory Committee that assisted in the final review of the manuscript prior to publication. The members of the Advisory Committee were Isaiah Frank, Michael L. Hoffman, John H. Ohly, Thomas C. Schelling, and Irving Swerdlow.

In preparing this study, the author also consulted with many other persons inside and outside the government who, without exception, responded generously and helpfully to his requests for information, advice, and assistance. The list includes, but is by no means limited to, Dragoslav Avramovic, Mary R. Banta, William R. Biggs, Kathleen Bitterman, Karl Bode, Richard N. Cooper, Paul Fisher, Irving S. Friedman, Theodore Geiger, David L. Gordon, Eugene S. Kerber,

John P. Lewis, I. G. Patel, Peter Ramm, Hale T. Shenefield, and Raymond Vernon.

Finally, there are certain members and former members of the Brookings staff to whom the author owes a special debt of gratitude, among them, Barbara Berke, Eleanor Busick, Richard Goode, H. Field Haviland, Jr., and Walter S. Salant. He feels deeply grateful also to Virginia Angel, who prepared the index and edited the manuscript.

The views expressed in the publication are those of the author and do not necessarily represent the views of those who were consulted during its preparation. Neither should they be construed as reflecting the views of the trustees, the officers, or other staff members of the Brookings Institution.

ROBERT D. CALKINS
President

March 1, 1961

Contents

	Page
FOREWORD	vii
INTRODUCTION	1
1. SOME TERMS DEFINED AND PRACTICES DESCRIBED	3
Grants and loans	6
Local currency transactions	7
How the firm supplying aid-financed goods gets paid	14
How the end-user of aid-financed goods makes payment	19
Who is really aided?	24
2. FOREIGN AID AND THE BALANCE OF PAYMENTS	26
Effects on United States balance of payments	28
Effects on balance of payments of aid-receiving countries	34
Effects on balance of payments of third countries	40
Recapitulation	42
3. TYPES AND AMOUNTS OF AID	46
Major foreign aid programs	46
Some expenditure figures and how to interpret them	55
Trends revealed by the figures	59
Aid receipts and income levels	65
Project and nonproject aid	67
4. POLICY ISSUES	78
How can country requirements for development aid be estimated?	79
Should development assistance be confined to loans?	91
Is there need for grant aid?	105

GRANTS, LOANS, AND LOCAL CURRENCIES

Which form of financing for which activities?......... 108
Translating country requirements into global
  requirements 113
Meeting global requirements........................ 118

5. SUMMARY AND CONCLUSIONS........................ 120
   Volume and distribution of aid..................... 121
   Local currency problems............................ 123
   Realities of foreign grants and loans................ 126
   Projects and programs.............................. 128
   Concluding caveats 133

SELECTED READINGS 137

INDEX 139

Introduction

MANY BASIC FACTS about foreign aid and the financial arrangements under which it has been—and can be—made available have been ignored or forgotten in the barrage of claims and counterclaims about "giveaways," "soft loans," "sound loans," and the practice of securing "double duty" from surplus commodities by "selling" them for local currencies and then using the proceeds for economic development or other purposes. Little, if any, systematic analysis has been made of the financial forms that American foreign aid has taken, can take, or should take. The grant/loan controversy has been dangerously oversimplified, and the discussion has been almost entirely in moral terms. Grants are bad and loans are good—or vice versa.

The key words have not been satisfactorily defined, the range of possibilities has not been systematically arrayed, and the relevant economic considerations have not been set forth in understandable form. This monograph therefore raises and seeks to answer four types of questions having to do, respectively, with concepts and procedures, magnitudes and trends, issues of public policy, and future courses of action:

1. Precisely what are we talking about? What are grants? What are loans? What are local currency transactions? What differences between them are revealed if we look beyond the formal agreement recording the transaction and ask how the firm supplying aid-financed goods gets paid and how the end-user in the foreign country makes payment? What are the effects of grants, hard loans, and soft loans on the balance of payments of the countries involved?

2. Under what authority and in what magnitudes has our Government been operating? What legal requirements have been imposed by the Mutual Security Acts, the Agricultural Trade Development and Assistance Act (Public Law 480) and its various amendments, and by other legislation governing the extension of foreign grants

and credits during the postwar period? What trends with respect to the grant and loan technique are revealed by the available data?

3. How has the United States accumulated its holdings of foreign currencies? What are the prospects for further accumulations? Can the granting or lending of local currencies serve as a substitute for dollar aid? If local currencies are not a substitute for dollar aid, what are they good for?

4. How can requirements for development aid be ascertained? Should loans be the preferred form for meeting requirements? Are some countries reaching the limits of their debt-servicing capacity? Is there a need for grant aid? Which type of project or program should be financed by which form of aid?

A search for answers to the foregoing questions should improve our understanding of foreign aid problems even though, at the end of the exploration, a number of equally fundamental questions may remain unanswered. This study does not deal directly with issues such as the objectives of American foreign assistance and their validity, the success in achieving stated objectives, the future scale of the program, or its duration. For the time being, the author accepts as fact that the United States is deeply involved in something generally known as the "foreign aid program," that aid is available for a wide range of projects, that some types of aid are more essential than others, and that the more meaningful types of assistance will continue in being for at least a few years to come—and probably for much longer.

1

Some Terms Defined and Practices Described

ALTHOUGH NO CLUSTER of governmental activities is formally designated as the "Foreign Aid Program," the term itself persists. The Congress does not pass foreign aid acts; its passes European Cooperation Acts, International Development Acts, Agricultural Trade Development and Assistance Acts, and similar measures. In recent years the mutual security legislation has, in congressional parlance, been the "foreign aid bill." The President has never established an agency called the Foreign Aid Administration, but the press and the public frequently refer to the International Cooperation Administration as the "foreign aid agency."

The term "foreign aid" has been employed loosely to encompass a variety of economic, military, technical, and humanitarian activities. The mixture has changed as the international environment, or the American appraisal thereof, has changed. The aid programs have been justified at different times and by different groups on different grounds. They have included at least three totally different major undertakings: rehabilitating and reconstructing the economies of war-devastated nations, strengthening and subsidizing the military defenses of the free world, and promoting economic growth and political stability in underdeveloped areas. In addition, aid programs have served, and still serve, to provide famine and disaster relief, to help eradicate malaria and other widely prevalent diseases, to provide budget and balance-of-payments support for friendly governments, and to perform a variety of other services considered to be in the interests of United States foreign policy.

The phrase "foreign aid" is encrusted with value judgments. Because it connotes action *for* rather than *with* others, it appears inappropriate to many who favor aid programs but prefer to accent the cooperation that is essential if aid is to be effectively used. They seek to popularize such terms as "mutual assistance," "mutual security," and "technical cooperation" to identify the programs. Their sensitivity and their concern with semantics lead them also to favor referring to the foreign government as the "host country" or "participating country" rather than the "recipient country."

Those opposed to foreign aid like to use the phrase precisely because it so often does connote unrequited action. In phrases such as "billions in foreign aid," it also conveys an impression of generosity and open handedness. As an image of America abroad, the impression may be an asset, but at home it can become a liability. A legislator may be admired both at home and abroad for generosity in disposing of his own resources, but he cannot command universal admiration for exercising this trait with respect to his constituents' resources.

The apparent common denominator of the aid programs is that, through them, other countries are enabled to obtain "essential" equipment, supplies, services, or reserves over and above the volume they would obtain in the normal course of trade or as a result of private investment, private remittances, and the expenditures of American tourists during the period in question. "Over and above normal acquisitions" implies that there is an element of subsidy in the transaction, which has to be provided through the intermediary of a public agency. Since the European economy began surging forward once more under its own momentum, it has been widely thought that the beneficiaries of the subsidy should be the so-called underdeveloped, or less industrialized, countries.

The term "foreign aid" nevertheless remains fuzzy. Aid of vital importance can be given with no drain on the public treasury. In the situation prevalent at the end of World War II, for example, when demand for foodstuffs was outrunning supply, our acquiescence in an international allocation system enabled participating countries to buy commodities that would otherwise have been impossible for them to procure at "reasonable" prices, if at all. Thus, even nations that paid "in full" were being aided, roughly to the tune of the difference between the amount they would have had to pay in an uncontrolled, competitive scramble and the amount they paid under the allocation system.

Even where substantial federal expenditures are involved, lines tend to be drawn arbitrarily. An American expenditure that permits additional Turkish troops to be mobilized and paid for their services is considered military aid to Turkey; but the payment of American troops stationed in Turkey shows up in the federal budget as one of the costs of operating the United States defense establishment, and the money such troops spend abroad enters our balance-of-payments accounts in somewhat the same manner as the expenditures of American tourists in Turkey.

Private institutions at times join with government agencies in extending credit to a foreign borrower. Even though the sums advanced by the private institutions would not otherwise have been forthcoming, such sums are not usually regarded as foreign aid. On the other hand, the full amount of the public portion is ordinarily thought of as aid until repaid, although one might argue with some cogency that, in public lending, the amount of aid extended is, in reality, equal only to the difference in interest payments resulting from the rate charged by the government and the rate that would have been charged had the loan been made through ordinary commercial channels. But what would have been the rate of interest on commercial loans to Asia during the early postwar years? If the commercial rate would have been prohibitively high, is it not appropriate to consider the principal also as aid?

The funds that public lending agencies raise by bond and portfolio sales to private American investors tend, when loaned abroad, to be regarded as foreign aid because it is the public agency that makes the foreign loan. However, the funds that go abroad under guaranties of the United States Government against risks such as inconvertibility of earnings or principal and loss through expropriation, confiscation, or war (and, in a few cases, guaranteed repayment of a loan to an underdeveloped country against virtually all risks) are regarded as private investment. If, as is recommended by some groups, the Investment Guaranty Program is expanded to make greater use of repayment guaranties and to include also so-called replacement guaranties (guaranties of equity investments made from accumulated earnings or reserves of American companies in underdeveloped areas), the potential cost to the United States Government will increase, and the lines between private investment and public foreign aid programs may be further blurred.

To avoid using the words "foreign aid" in a publication such as this would be more pedantic than to use the expression from time to time (despite its connotations and limitations) as the generic term for a congeries of governmental programs through which funds and goods and services, additional to those normally acquired, are made available to other nations.

Grants and Loans

Aid may be given as a grant—a transfer of resources with no obligation concerning repayment. The grant may be in commodities, services, dollars, or currencies other than dollars. These same items may be loaned instead of granted—that is, furnished by the lender on the understanding that they will in due course be paid for by the borrower. The loan can be long-term, medium-term, or short-term. It can be interest-free or interest-bearing. Repayment of principal can begin promptly or after a period of grace. To either a loan or a grant, special conditions concerning receipt and use may be attached.

The classic and fundamental difference between a loan and a grant seems too obvious to belabor: a loan has to be repaid, a grant does not. The recipient of a loan obtains something of value, and over time makes a return of corresponding value. The recipient of a grant obtains something of value without having to yield anything of corresponding value. Repayment of a loan requires an act of saving, of discipline, of self-denial. A grant requires only courteous acknowledgment.

Under American foreign assistance programs of the postwar period, however, the "strings" that have been tied to grants and the leeway given with respect to loans have tended to obscure some of the distinctions between them. The key to an understanding of the changes that have occurred lies partly in fuller knowledge of the role assigned to local currencies in the various programs.

Local Currency Transactions

Local currency transactions involve the accumulation and disposition of foreign currencies that are either owned by the United States Government as a result of its foreign economic operations or over which the United States Government exercises some degree of control. The sources and authorized uses of the various local currency accounts are well described in some recent congressional hearings from which the following section borrows heavily.[1]

The four major categories of foreign money deposits are officially known as counterpart funds, Public Law 480 local currency, Section 402 currencies, and foreign currency repayments.

Counterpart Funds

Counterpart funds have figured in foreign aid programs throughout the postwar period, beginning with the United Nations Relief and Rehabilitation Administration (UNRRA). The Economic Cooperation Act of 1948 (launching the Marshall Plan) required foreign governments receiving grant aid from the United States to deposit in a special account a commensurate amount of their own money, which would represent the counterpart of the dollar aid received. The successor Mutual Security Acts require that, when certain economic aid appropriations are used by the United States to finance grants of commodities, the recipient country deposit in the counterpart account, not the full equivalent of the grant, but the local

[1] Memorandum submitted for the record by C. Douglas Dillon, Under Secretary of State for Economic Affairs, in *Mutual Security Appropriations for 1960 (and Related Agencies)*, Hearings before House Committee on Appropriations, May 26, 1959, 86 Cong. 1 sess., pp. 364-76. Hereafter referred to as Dillon Memorandum.

currency proceeds which the recipient government derives from sales of the commodities to its own nationals. Although the Mutual Security Acts make the policy mandatory only with respect to the type of economic aid known as defense support, the general practice of the International Cooperation Administration (ICA) is to require counterpart deposits on any grant of nonmilitary commodity aid which generates proceeds for the recipient government. Congress has clearly indicated that it expects ICA to follow such a policy.[2]

Behind the congressional expectation has been the desire that commercial channels of trade be used to the maximum extent possible, except for military hardware transferred directly to the defense establishment of the receiving country. Goods should not be given free to business establishments and individuals able to pay for them merely because their government feels unable to release foreign exchange for the purchase. If they were distributed free, some firms would enjoy an unfair competitive advantage, some individuals would receive undeservedly favorable treatment, and duplicate channels of distribution would have to be established for many commodities. Logic seemed to dictate that most aid-financed commodities should be paid for by end-users.

The requirement that the local currency proceeds of sales, or a sum commensurate with the dollar assistance received, be deposited in a special account from which expenditures could be made only with the concurrence of the United States had the further objective of deterring inflation and helping to stabilize the internal economy of the participating country. Inflation was rampant in Europe in 1948. The anti-inflationary contribution of the Marshall Plan, it was expected, would be to increase the flow of goods into the economy without correspondingly increasing the money supply. Instead, purchasing power would be mopped up through temporarily sterilizing a sum equivalent to the proceeds of the sale of the imported commodities. The local currency thus mobilized, it was argued at

[2] Memorandum of July 1, 1958, from John G. Burnett, Associate General Counsel of ICA, in Robert L. Berenson, William M. Bristol, and Ralph I. Strauss, *Accumulation and Administration of Local Currencies*, a Special Report to James H. Smith, Jr., Director, ICA, August 1958, Annex B, pp. 60-69. Hereafter referred to as Burnett Memorandum.

the inception of the Marshall Plan, could make a further contribution to economic stability if subsequently employed to stimulate particular lines of production.

Counterpart accounts are owned by the depositing country. A small portion (commonly referred to as "10 per cent counterpart") is normally turned over to the United States for use in paying United States expenses in that country. It is deposited in a United States-owned account controlled by the Treasury Department. The 10 per cent counterpart can be used by United States Government agencies only (with some minor exceptions) by purchasing it from the United States Treasury with appropriated dollars.[3]

Strictly speaking, it is only the balance of the counterpart (90 per cent counterpart) that is owned by the other country. It is available solely for uses agreed to by the United States. With respect to counterpart generated through mutual security appropriations, United States concurrence is limited by law to expenditures designed to promote the purposes of the Mutual Security Act, including economic development, budgetary needs, and military requirements.

Under the authority of Title II of the Agricultural Trade Development and Assistance Act (Public Law 83-480, as amended), the United States Government may make grants of surplus agricultural commodities to relieve famine or other urgent or extraordinary needs and, to a limited extent, to promote economic development. The law does not require the country receiving commodities under this authority to deposit counterpart funds, but where such commodities generate proceeds for the country, the ICA as a matter of policy has generally required such proceeds to be deposited in a counterpart account from which expenditures may be made only with the concurrence of the United States. The United States cannot legally compel foreign governments to spend counterpart if they do not wish to do so.

The issues raised by these policies will be discussed later. The view that the counterpart procedure increases the effectiveness of American foreign aid rests on the belief that consultation with the United States will result in decisions more favorable to economic recovery, stability, development, or defense "than would have been

[3] *Ibid.*, p. 61.

the case without American intervention. This belief obviously involves questions of both fact and judgment in each case." [4]

The main point to be made here is that grant aid is not a pure gift on which the books are closed after receipt of the commodities granted. Up to about one tenth of it may result in a "reverse grant" to the United States, and the handling of the remainder frequently, but not always, requires international collaboration similar to that required in connection with intergovernmental loans.

Public Law 480 Local Currency

Of the various programs resulting in deposits of foreign money, by far the largest at the present time are the deposits acquired by the United States Government in return for sales of surplus agricultural commodities pursuant to Title I of Public Law 480. Public Law 480 was conceived as a surplus disposal program rather than as a foreign aid program, but it has rapidly become an important form of assistance to friendly countries. The basic purpose of the law is—

> to enable the United States to transfer a part of its surpluses of agricultural commodities out of our burdensome stocks into consumption channels in foreign countries which are not in a position to pay for them with foreign exchange, that is in dollars or convertible currencies. Public Law 480 gets around these foreign balance-of-payments difficulties by authorizing the U.S. Government to accept inconvertible local currencies in exchange for U.S. agricultural surpluses. The result is that the United States is enabled to export a larger volume of its surpluses than would otherwise be possible and foreign countries are able to import and consume more agricultural products than they could otherwise pay for.[5]

The proceeds of the sales—Public Law 480 currencies—can be used for three major purposes:

(1) for the recipient country, mainly as loans and grants for economic development and as grants for military purposes;
(2) for loans to private American and, in certain cases, foreign enterprises (so-called Cooley amendment loans); and

---

[4] William Adams Brown, Jr., and Redvers Opie, *American Foreign Assistance*, (The Brookings Institution, 1953), p. 243.
[5] Dillon Memorandum, p. 367.

(3) for the United States Government, including administrative expenses within the country, agricultural marketing programs, international educational exchange, and other purposes specified by law.[6]

With respect to United States uses, the act provides that not less than 10 per cent of the currencies under Title I shall be available to pay United States obligations abroad. To the extent needed, the currencies may be purchased by United States Government agencies for dollars from the United States Treasury.[7]

The Cooley amendment to Public Law 480, adopted in 1957, requires that up to 25 per cent of P.L. 480 foreign currencies be made available for lending to private American enterprise for use in foreign countries or to foreign business firms which help expand markets for United States agricultural products. The currencies are made available to the Export-Import Bank, which lends them to private firms.

Unlike counterpart funds, which are owned by the countries that receive grant aid, Public Law 480 local currencies are owned by the United States Government, including the portion which has been set aside for the use of the recipient country under the terms of loans and grants. Transfers from the United States account to the account of the recipient country do not take place until the recipient country actually draws against the account to cover expenditures financed under agreed loans or grants. Pending disbursement, the United States holding may earn interest from the foreign bank in which it has been deposited.

The differences between foreign-owned counterpart accounts and United States-owned P.L. 480 local currencies, though legally and politically important, are largely a matter of historical accident and are not of immediate economic importance. Counterpart funds had their birth in programs designed to aid friendly countries that were in need. Since such countries could no longer spend foreign exchange for the commodities they required, the United States did not ask for payment. It gave the commodities (including a very substantial volume of agricultural commodities) as foreign aid and

[6] *Ibid.*, pp. 367-68.
[7] Burnett Memorandum, p. 66.

asked the recipient government to deposit in an account of its own the equivalent cost in its currency. P.L. 480 funds had their birth in programs designed to dispose of surplus agricultural commodities, despite the fact that dollar payment could not reasonably be expected. Giving the commodities away seemed politically less palatable than selling them for foreign currencies that would belong to the United States and lending, or even granting, the currencies to the country that had made the purchase.

It will be observed that, in both cases, the United States has parted with a real physical resource—the commodities in question. In both cases it receives payment, in real terms, for up to 10 per cent of the value of the transfer, through the portion of the counterpart or of the sales proceeds reserved for United States administrative uses. Additional payments, if any, are obtained in real terms only when additional goods and services are made available by the receiving country to the United States or to a third country designated by the United States—not when the country's own currency is deposited in an earmarked account. The earmarked accounts, whether comprised of the 90 per cent counterpart funds or the P.L. 480 funds reserved for loans and grants, may be drawn down only for uses agreed to by the United States and the recipient country.

Section 402 Currencies

Antedating and supplementing the provisions of P.L. 480 as a combination surplus disposal, foreign aid measure have been certain provisions of the Mutual Security Act itself. The Congress, eager to develop constructive uses for our mounting agricultural surpluses, in 1953 inserted in the Mutual Security Act a provision (Section 550 of the Mutual Security Act of 1951, as amended) requiring that, during the fiscal year 1954, not less than $100 million of the funds appropriated for foreign aid be used to buy surplus agricultural products which could be sold abroad for foreign currencies. The foreign currency sales were not to displace or substitute for usual marketings from the United States or friendly countries, and prices were to be in line with world market prices.

Similar provisions specifying that larger sums be so used have been included in subsequent acts (Section 402 of the Mutual Security Act of 1954, as amended) and the currencies acquired are known as Section 402 currencies. The specification that sales be in addition to usual marketings has been dropped, however.

Like Public Law 480 local currencies, Section 402 currencies are owned by the United States Government. They differ from Public Law 480 currencies, however, in that they must be used exclusively to assist countries receiving aid under the Mutual Security Act. Normally they are promptly programmed on a grant basis for the use and benefit of those countries, but they may also be loaned to them. There is no requirement that 10 per cent, or any other proportion, be set aside for the use of United States agencies.

Foreign Currency Repayments

The United States acquires foreign currencies not only in payment for sales of surplus commodities but also in repayment of loans that are made from the proceeds of such sales. Moreover, dollar loans may, in certain cases, be repaid in the currency of the borrowing country. The Development Loan Fund (DLF), for example, is authorized to receive foreign currencies in repayment of dollar loans extended to a foreign country by the DLF, and to use the repayment for relending.[8] The International Cooperation Administration is also authorized to make dollar loans repayable in local currency.

Repayments in foreign currencies of either dollar loans or local currency loans are deposited in various United States-owned accounts and subject to different restrictions, depending on the statutory authorization under which the loan was made. It should be borne in mind from the outset, however, that, as a result of interest charges to borrowers, plus interest collected on undisbursed portions of our deposits in foreign banks, the United States accumulation of foreign currencies can ultimately exceed by a considerable sum the amount originally received in return for surplus commodities or dollar exchange. Moreover, under DLF and ICA procedures governing local currency repayment of dollar loans, the borrower must agree to a maintenance-of-value clause preserving the dollar value of the original loan. If the country subsequently devalues its currency, the quantity of that currency owed to the DLF or the ICA

[8] Dillon Memorandum, p. 376.

increases proportionately. Until early 1959, loans of local currency under P.L. 480 also carried maintenance-of-value clauses.

Soft Loans

Loans made on the theory that full repayment in a convertible currency, although not necessarily out of the question, is too uncertain to be made a condition of the loan, are frequently called "soft loans." The term "soft loan," however, may embrace not only loans repayable partially or wholly in inconvertible currencies, but also loans repayable in dollars on longer terms or at lower rates of interest or with more generous periods of grace before principal repayments begin than the "hard loans" of the "conventional lending agencies." Rapid change being a hallmark of the day, the International Bank for Reconstruction and Development and the Export-Import Bank of Washington are now classed as conventional lending agencies, though a few years ago their activities were considered well outside the pale of conventionality.

To summarize: The various local currency accounts connected with foreign aid operations are built up pursuant to agreements with countries that receive from the United States something of immediate value—agricultural or other commodities, or a claim on dollars. To the modest extent that the accounts are then drawn down by the United States for its own administrative expenses or for other uses that would ordinarily require dollar expenditures, payment is obtained in real terms. Regarding the balance, the economic validity of a distinction between portions loaned and portions granted depends on the extent to which the loan portion is ultimately converted into goods and services of value to the United States.

How the Firm Supplying Aid-Financed Goods Gets Paid

Whether aid takes the form of a grant, a hard loan, or a soft loan makes little difference to the firm supplying the aid-financed goods. The American producer of locomotives or lard, pumps or pills, does not normally give away his product and does not wish to deviate unnecessarily from standard commercial procedure. With rare exceptions, he expects to be paid in dollars. Precisely how is this accomplished?

There are variations, of course, between the procedures of the International Cooperation Administration, the Development Loan Fund, the Export-Import Bank, and other agencies. Moreover, no agency follows an identical procedure in every situation. Let us look first at the customary ICA procedure, as outlined to a congressional subcommittee in mid-1958.[9]

ICA Procedures

The ICA acts as a financing agency rather than a procurement agency. It issues what are called letters of commitment to United States banks. The banks, on instruction from the cooperating country, open letters of credit in favor of the supplying companies. After certain documents have been submitted by the suppliers, the banks pay them and the ICA reimburses the banks.

To illustrate, let us assume that a decision has been made by ICA to make a $1 million grant available to Korea to finance imports of wheat flour. The decision would be reflected in a document (the procurement authorization) issued by ICA to the Government of the Republic of Korea. The latter would then inform importers in Korea that it has the $1 million grant in ICA funds and would ask interested importers of wheat flour to apply for import licenses.

As a result, the ABC Company of Seoul might receive a license, together with a commitment from the Korean Government that it would make available $100,000 in foreign (dollar) exchange. (In this manner, the Government of Korea might subdivide the ICA authorization of $1 million among 10 or more private Korean importers.) *The ABC Company would solicit offers from American exporters just as it would if ICA were not involved.* Should the

[9] The next few paragraphs, except as noted, have been taken almost verbatim from a statement by Marvin A. Bacon, Office of the Controller, ICA, in *Investigation of the Commodity Credit Corporation,* Hearings before House Committee on Government Operations, July 2, 1958, 85 Cong. 2 sess., pp. 80-81.

most attractive offer be received from the XYZ Company of Boston, the ABC Company of Seoul would request that a letter of credit be opened in favor of the XYZ Company by the Sixth National Bank of New York.

The ICA would issue the Sixth National Bank a "letter of commitment" agreeing to reimburse the bank for payments made under the letter of credit opened in compliance with the United States obligation to the Republic of Korea. When the XYZ Company of Boston became ready to ship to the Korean importer, it would present the usual commercial documents to the Sixth National Bank and receive payment from the bank.

There are safeguards all along the line to ensure that the commodities and the services financed by ICA have actually been provided. Before the Sixth National Bank paid the XYZ Company for the goods delivered to the ABC Company, it would have received a series of basic documents, including the supplier's certificate (wherein the supplier makes certain certifications with reference to price, commissions, and related data), bills of lading, delivery receipts, and invoices. The bank would then send these papers to the ICA and the ICA would reimburse the bank.[10]

On the Korean side, the Korean importer pays to the Korean bank the hwan equivalent of $100,000. The $100,000 in hwan collected by the Korean bank would become part of the counterpart fund, available for uses mutually agreed by the United States and the Republic of Korea.

Insofar as the incentives of both buyer and seller are concerned, the fact that ICA may be providing the dollar exchange in the form of a grant is of no importance. The XYZ Company in Boston will offer wheat flour at a price that will not only meet the tests established by ICA regulations, but will win business in a competitive world. The ABC Company in Seoul will bargain to buy as cheaply as possible because its business life depends on its ability to sell at a profit against local competition in the Korean market.[11]

[10] Testimony of Leslie Grant, Office of the General Counsel, ICA, July 17, 1958, *ibid.*, p. 106.

[11] The above example may exaggerate somewhat the extent of competition in certain underdeveloped countries in which the business community is small, the inflow of foreign aid substantial, and the government more partial to some local enterprises than to others.

In addition to the "letter of commitment" procedure, the ICA may employ what it calls the "direct reimbursement" procedure. In such cases, the country receiving the aid finances the transaction initially and then presents ICA with documents enabling it to reimburse the country for the outlays made. This procedure does not involve the use of the banks. It is rarely employed, however, principally because most of the aid-receiving nations do not have the money to finance the transactions initially.

DLF Procedures

Let us assume now that, instead of a grant from ICA, Korea has received a loan from the Development Loan Fund. Would it then receive $1 million to deposit and expend with fewer and different controls? The short answer is "no." In accordance with what has become the established practice of public lending institutions, the Development Loan Fund would not disburse the entire amount of the loan to the borrower at the time the loan agreement was signed. Instead, it would follow procedures almost identical to those of ICA, disbursing the proceeds of the loan, as required for specific purposes, through either of two methods.

Under its "letter of commitment" procedure, the DLF addresses a letter of commitment to any American bank of the borrower's choosing, in which the DLF agrees to reimburse the bank for any monies paid by it at the direction of the borrower for those items of equipment, materials, or supplies described in the letter of commitment. Under the "reimbursement procedure" of the DLF, the borrower pays for the goods and services to be financed and is then reimbursed by the DLF upon presenting proof of having made the expenditures for the purposes and under the conditions of the loan. The reimbursement procedure is normally employed in those cases where payments are due so many different suppliers that the letter of commitment procedure is not practicable.[12]

Procedures of the Export-Import Bank

The Export-Import Bank prides itself on tailoring its procedures to the needs of the occasion. Like the DLF, it uses the reimburse-

---

[12] *Development Loan Fund,* June 1959, pp. 11-12.

ment procedure, particularly for the smaller items required by a foreign borrower. At times it has employed a revolving-fund procedure whereby it places a limited sum at the disposal of a foreign borrower, which it replenishes upon evidence that earlier disbursements were made for agreed purposes. For major equipment, the foreign borrower, having already had preliminary negotiations with the United States supplier, would tell the Export-Import Bank which American commercial bank it, the foreign borrower, would prefer to deal with. It might ask the Export-Import Bank to guarantee its letter of credit in favor of the United States supplier. The Export-Import Bank would then inform the commercial bank that it had made a loan to the foreign corporation or other entity and that it stood ready and willing to guarantee its letter of credit. The American bank, secure in the knowledge that it could look to the Export-Import Bank for payment of goods purchased against the letter of credit, would open the letter in favor of the United States supplier for payment according to the schedule agreed between the foreign purchaser and the American supplier.

The American supplier, upon evidence of having fulfilled his part of the bargain, would be paid by the bank in dollars in the same fashion as for any other international commercial transaction. The commercial bank would look either to the Export-Import Bank or to the foreign corporation for reimbursement, and the Export-Import Bank would debit the foreign borrower's note by the amount of the transaction.

World Bank Procedures

Unlike the ICA, the DLF, and the Export-Import Bank, the International Bank for Reconstruction and Development (known also as the World Bank and the IBRD) is not an agency of the United States Government. It is a multilateral agency with access to a number of different currencies. Furthermore, its borrowers are free to use their loan proceeds for purchases on the best possible terms in any of its 66 member countries and in Switzerland. It consequently can, and normally does, disburse its loans in the currencies in which equipment and services will have to be paid for. The Bank can furnish the currency needed either by drawing on currencies it owns or by buying the needed currency. In the first case the borrower repays the loan in the currency which it receives from the Bank; in the second case the loan is repaid in the currency which the Bank has used to purchase the necessary currency.

The International Bank normally disburses funds only as expenditures are incurred for the project being financed. It can reimburse the borrower for such expenditures or it can, when requested by the borrower, pay American and other suppliers of equipment directly. It can also guarantee reimbursement to commercial banks under letters of credit in favor of designated suppliers. Most of its loans have been made for the development of basic services such as electric power and transport. Loans may be made either to a member government or directly to private or public enterprises under a governmental guaranty of repayment.

American suppliers of aid-financed goods thus receive their payment in dollars irrespective of whether aid to the foreign country takes the form of a grant from ICA, a loan repayable in local currency from the DLF, or a loan repayable in dollars from the Export-Import Bank or from a multilateral agency such as the World Bank. Just as the private exporter would find it necessary to vary his procedure somewhat in executing transactions on private account, he will find situations on public account in which payment is made to him by a private bank and other situations in which it is made by the public lending agency. The differences are due to legal requirements and administrative policies; they do *not* grow out of inherent differences between grants and loans or between hard loans and soft loans.

How the End-User of Aid-Financed Goods Makes Payment

It is perhaps obvious that American suppliers of aid-financed goods must be paid promptly and preferably in dollars for their services, but it is not equally obvious, especially with respect to grant aid, that the end-user in the foreign country must make payment for what he receives. Perhaps it would be useful to supplement the earlier hypothetical example of relations between the

ABC Company of Seoul and the XYZ Company of Boston with some actual examples.

An Export-Import Bank Loan

In February 1958, for instance, the Export-Import Bank of Washington authorized a credit of $150 million to the Government of India to assist in financing the acquisition in the United States and the export to India of coal-mining machinery, steel-working equipment, and other capital goods required for development projects, both public and private. (The Export-Import Bank normally makes "tied loans," that is, loans usable only for purchases in the country making the loan; hence the requirement that the equipment be obtained in the United States.)

India is one of a number of countries that still maintains exchange controls. Upon completion of the loan agreement, therefore, Indian importers were notified by their government that licenses for the import of the equipment covered by the loan agreement would be granted. Importers obtaining licenses take them to their respective banks as evidence that the government is prepared to release the necessary foreign exchange. These banks, through American banks of their choosing, open letters of credit in favor of designated American suppliers. On the basis of these letters of credit, the American suppliers get paid in dollars upon evidence of having fulfilled their commitments. The Indian importer pays for the dollar exchange in Indian rupees, the only currency in which he does business. The rupee account he maintains at his bank is consequently reduced and the rupees are used by his bank to pay the Government of India, through its central bank, for the requisite number of dollars. The Government of India then releases an equivalent number of dollars, acquired by debiting its note at the Export-Import Bank. For the time being, India's foreign exchange reserves remain unchanged because it will have simply drawn on its line of credit for the dollar cost of the equipment.

The loan is repayable over a 10-year period commencing in 1964, and interest is due at the rate of 5¼ per cent per annum. In a case such as this, it is not the importer of the equipment who pays 5¼ per cent interest, for he receives no special financial accommodation; he pays for the equipment in rupees on delivery.[13] Payments of interest to the Export-Import Bank, when due, and repayments of principal are the responsibility of the Government of India—and will reduce its foreign exchange reserves.

A DLF Loan

Whereas the loans of the Export-Import Bank are normally repayable in dollars, the Development Loan Fund has made a series of loans to the Government of India repayable in rupees. The $40 million railway expansion and modernization loan made in June 1958 is an example. It is repayable over a 20-year period, with interest at 3½ per cent. The loan is intended to finance—

> the importation of structural steel and other steel products to be used in the manufacture of railroad freight cars and coaches and steam locomotives for use on the Indian railway system. The steel acquired from the proceeds of this loan will be utilized by private manufacturers and government-owned facilities to produce approximately 20,000 freight cars, 300 steam locomotives, 600 steel coaches, and 2,500 underframes. The loan will complement an extensive railroad improvement project being undertaken by the Government of India under loans extended to it by the International Bank for Reconstruction and Development.[14]

Government-owned facilities will not benefit without cost. The Indian railways, like those of most other countries, are government owned, but they operate under a budget of their own. This budget is debited the rupee value of equipment received as a result of the DLF loan. If the capital equipment acquired in a particular year exceeds what the railways can pay for from their available resources, the railway system may have to negotiate a loan from the Government of India, but any such loan would be of no direct concern to the DLF.

---

[13] To be sure, he may have negotiated a loan with his own bank in order to make the payment, but such a transaction would not directly concern the Government of India or the Export-Import Bank of Washington. The rate of interest he paid might be more, or less, than 5¼ per cent.

[14] Development Loan Fund, *Fiscal Year 1960 Estimates*, p. 48.

A World Bank Loan

Although the Development Loan Fund has also made loans to India to finance the purchase of capital equipment for private industries, perhaps the best-known public loans to private industry in India are those by the International Bank to the Tata Iron and Steel Company, Ltd. The first such loan was made in 1956 for $75 million at 4¾ per cent, and the second in 1957 for $32.5 million at 6 per cent. In accordance with the articles of agreement of the International Bank, these loans, though made to a private corporation, are guaranteed by the Government of India.

The loans made by the IBRD are not tied to supply sources in particular member countries. The Tata Company is expected to prepare its own specifications, to make its own approaches to suppliers, wherever they may be, to solicit bids, and to enter directly into contracts for equipment that meets the specifications. As deliveries of equipment are made, the Tata Company may go to its bank (presumably an authorized commercial bank in India), pay over the rupee equivalent of the dollars or other foreign currencies that are due at the time, and ask that the necessary foreign exchange be released. The Indian Government, which has guaranteed the loan, would consider itself bound to approve the request and release the necessary foreign exchange. Alternatively, the Tata Company could, as previously indicated, arrange with the IBRD for release of the necessary foreign exchange from its loan account for the purpose of paying the supplier.

Whereas a large private enterprise in India, or an autonomous public authority such as the Commissioners of the Port of Calcutta, would be expected to negotiate directly with foreign producers for the equipment it needed, purchases for regular government agencies are handled by the Ministry of Works, Housing, and Supply in somewhat the same way that the General Services Administration buys for United States Government departments. The branch of the Ministry of Works, Housing, and Supply that makes purchases in the United States is the Indian Supply Mission in Washington.

The commodities received by India as grant aid are normally sold for rupees in the same manner as those whose import is made possible by loan aid. The proceeds of such sales may be used for a variety of purposes, including loans to Indian enterprises. Several years ago, for example, a grant of steel from the United States Foreign Operations Administration (a predecessor of the ICA) was sold in India for rupees. The rupees obtained by the Indian Government as counterpart were then used to finance its subscription to a new domestic development institution, the Industrial Credit and Investment Corporation of India. A local financial institution, it was felt, would be better equipped than a United States or United Nations agency to investigate the credit-worthiness of, and to extend credit to, private domestic enterprises.

The corporation, established in early 1955 to facilitate the growth of private industry, is a complex financial partnership illustrative of the way in which foreign capital obtained in the form of grants, loans, and private investments can be pooled with local capital to serve as the basis for a loan program in the receiving country.

> Of the initial share capital, amounting to 50 million rupees ($10.5 million), 35 million rupees were subscribed by Indian investors; 10 million rupees were subscribed by British investors (the Eastern Exchange Banks, several insurance companies and industrial firms, and the Commonwealth Development Finance Company, Ltd.); and 5 million rupees were subscribed by United States investors (Bank of America, the Rockefeller brothers, Olin Mathieson Chemical Corp. and Westinghouse Electric International Corporation). In addition, the Indian Government made a long-term, interest-free advance to the Corporation of 75 million rupees drawn from counterpart funds generated by United States aid [i.e., the previously mentioned grant of steel].[15]

Additional loan capital was provided by the International Bank in the form of a fifteen-year loan of $10 million at 4⅝ per cent interest, with amortization to begin after a five-year period of grace.

It would be incorrect to leave the impression that end-users of aid-financed commodities and equipment always pay in local currency for what they get. DDT for malaria control, for example, is received by the Government of India as a grant and distributed free as a public health measure. Obviously, this case is different from the case in which the aid-financed imports are destined for a steel plant which would enjoy an unfair advantage over its competitors

[15] International Bank for Reconstruction and Development, *Tenth Annual Report, 1954-1955, Appendices*, p. 30.

if it were exempted from paying the rupee cost of the equipment it received.

Because the steel plant does pay the rupee cost, however, its owners, although they acquire something of value that they probably could not otherwise import, may not feel grateful to the United States, particularly if a requirement that the loan be expended only in the United States raises the rupee cost above what it would be under world-wide competitive bidding. One of the ironies of the foreign aid business, truer in the Marshall Plan period than today, is that the receiver of equipment, having paid for it, does not consider himself an aid recipient and resents the implication that he owes some special debt of gratitude to the United States. At the same time, his competitors, thinking that he probably was subsidized in some way and knowing full well that they were not, may also be resentful. To top it off, the American steel producer may be irritated with the United States Government for having facilitated an improvement in the competitive position of some foreign rivals, and with the rivals for their failure to be grateful.

Analysis of procurement and payment procedures makes it clear that it is more or less immaterial to the American supplier and to the Indian purchaser of locomotives, lard, or other aid-financed transfers whether the transaction at the governmental level is a loan repayable in dollars, a loan repayable in rupees, or a grant. Some special forms and records may be prescribed, but purchaser and seller can usually deal directly with each other. The purchaser has all the usual incentives to buy only what he needs and to expend the minimum number of rupees in doing so, and the seller has the same incentives to sell what he can and obtain the dollars needed to remain in business.

Who Is Really Aided?

If the normal procedure under economic aid programs is for the consumer in the receiving country to pay the going price in local currency for what he gets, one may legitimately ask how he can be demoralized by foreign aid. The aid may have enabled him to enlarge the volume of his business or helped him indirectly but, as far as he is concerned, there has been no giveaway, no soft loan, no significant deviation from normal commercial practice.

The prime beneficiary of foreign aid is usually the government of the receiving country. It has the local currency in a counterpart account if the aid came in grant form. It often has access to the local currency in a United States-owned account, through re-borrowing, if the aid came in the form of a loan repayable in the currency of the borrower. It may have the use of some additional local currency prior to the time that it has to release the equivalent in foreign exchange, if the aid took the form of a loan repayable in the currency of the lender. It has the capital goods, if the aid took the form of tanks, planes, or road-building equipment not sold or transferred to other end-users within the receiving country.

If the government benefits by increasing its resources without having to levy additional taxes, and if it is a government dedicated to the promotion of the general welfare, the people will benefit too —some more than others.[16] The farmers in newly irrigated areas can expect to be better off, even though they pay their pro rata share of the water they use. The patrons of a modernized railway system should get more for their money. Borrowers from a properly run development bank will have a good chance of earning more than enough to repay their loans.

In the aid-giving country, as in the receiving country, there are benefits as well as costs, and both may be inequitably distributed. Some producers may greatly increase their sales, while others lose markets they formerly enjoyed. The particular type of financing agreed upon at the government level—grant, soft loan, or hard loan —is of little direct significance to sellers in the aid-giving nation or to buyers in the aid-receiving nation. The aid-receiving government can sell commodities that it receives on a grant basis. It can, though it usually does not, give away commodities for which it has to pay. It can use either grant or loan aid, or both, to establish a lending institution within its boundaries. In short, there is no necessary connection between the form of the intergovernmental transaction and the financial terms on which the capital or the commodities obtained subsequently become available to business enterprises and private citizens in the country aided.

[16] See Thomas C. Schelling, *International Economics* (Allyn and Bacon, Inc., 1958), pp. 425-26.

2

Foreign Aid and the Balance of Payments

ALTHOUGH THE PARTICULAR TYPE of financing agreed upon between governments is of little direct importance to the firm that supplies aid-financed goods or to the end-user of the goods, it has a bearing on the balance of payments and the international financial position of the nations concerned. What are these balance-of-payments effects, not only on the United States and the aid-receiving country but also, in certain instances, on third countries?

Before seeking to answer this question, it may be useful to try to dispel some of the confusion surrounding the balance-of-payments concept. Normally, the term "balance of payments" refers to a statement summarizing the major categories of receipts from abroad and payments made abroad by residents of the reporting nation during a given period of time. The difference between receipts and payments, however—the surplus or deficit—is also sometimes referred to as the "balance of payments."

Contrary to popular opinion, surpluses and deficits are no more indicative of increases or decreases in national wealth than changes in one's own bank balance are indicative of greater or lesser personal wealth. The man who draws down his bank balance in order to buy stocks, bonds, or a new home reduces his *liquid* assets but may in the process increase his *total* assets. Similarly, a nation may reduce its monetary reserves without diminishing its basic economic strength, or build them up without improving its over-all position.

As a tool of economic analysis, the balance of payments may be used in several ways. Writing in *The Economic Journal* in early

1950, Fritz Machlup, obviously nettled by loose talk about the dollar shortage, sought to distinguish three different concepts of the balance of payments: a market balance, a program balance, and an accounting balance.[1]

The market balance reflects the demand for and the supply of foreign exchange at the established rate of exchange or at alternative hypothetical rates. The program balance is a statement of the sources of and uses for foreign funds over a future period of one or more years, based on an official or unofficial estimate of the capital and consumption requirements of a nation and on a program for meeting an excess of requirements over resources. The accounting balance is a record of all economic transactions which have taken place over a past period of one or more years between the residents of a country and those of other countries, the record being kept in the form of double-entry bookkeeping, with each credit entry balanced by an offsetting debit entry, and vice versa.[2]

It follows that deficits in these balances have different meanings. A persistent deficit in the market balance of payments—an excessive amount of domestic money wanting to be exchanged into foreign money—indicates that the nation's monetary, fiscal, wage, and other policies affecting its international transactions are incompatible with the maintenance of its international liquid reserves at the existing foreign exchange rates. A persistent deficit in the program balance—repeated plans to liquidate foreign assets, to contract foreign debts, and to negotiate foreign grants—indicates a belief that it will be necessary for the nation to spend more on consumption and capital formation than the value of its output. A persistent deficit in the accounting balance indicates that the nation in the past has been able to draw on its reserves, dispose of its foreign assets and/or secure foreign loans and grants.[3]

Although the three concepts are probably not as separable as Professor Machlup assumes, they do differ and the distinctions are of value.

[1] "Three Concepts of the Balance of Payments and the So-Called Dollar Shortage," *The Economic Journal*, Vol. LX (March 1950), pp. 46-68.
[2] *Ibid.*, pp. 46-47.
[3] *Ibid.*, p. 67.

Effects on United States Balance of Payments

When the effects of foreign aid programs on the United States balance of payments are discussed in the publications of the aid-dispensing agencies, it is usually the accounting balance that is under review. A deficit in our accounting balance means that our total receipts from exports of goods and services and inflows of foreign long-term capital have been insufficient, *during the period in question,* to cover our total payments for imports of goods and services, our private capital outflow, and our governmental expenditures abroad. The deficit in liquid foreign assets—a decline in gold holdings less net short-term liabilities to foreigners—may be accompanied by an increase in total net foreign assets if the amount of long-term investment abroad, public and private, exceeds the amount of the deficit.

Immediate Effects

Foreign aid enters into the payments or outflow side of the account in the amounts extended and affects the receipts side by at least the portion thereof used to finance exports of goods and services of American origin. Grants of commodities and services of American origin are treated as though the receiving countries had been given the money with which to buy the commodities or services. Thus, a grant of American steel to India shows up on the outflow side of the account as a payment to India by the United States, a "unilateral transfer" of an amount equal to the value placed on the steel. The same sum shows up again on the inflow or receipts side of the account as earnings from the export of steel under the heading "merchandise exports." Grants of planes, tanks, and war materiel under military assistance programs show up on the inflow side under a separate heading as receipts from exports "transferred under military grants."[4]

If the goods and services financed by American aid would have been purchased from the United States anyhow, without correspondingly reducing foreign purchases of other American goods and services, then the outflow side of our account has been increased unnecessarily and the deficit in our balance of payments

[4] See Table I: United States Balance of Payments, 1956-60.

TABLE I. *United States Balance of Payments, 1956-60*
(In billions of dollars)[a]

	Type of Transaction	1956	1957	1958	1959	1960
1.	UNITED STATES RECEIPTS—TOTAL	27.9	31.0	26.5	27.8	28.8
2.	From exports of goods and services	26.3	29.2	25.6	25.5	28.8
3.	Transfers under military grants	2.6	2.4	2.3	2.0	1.7[b]
4.	Other goods and services	23.7	26.7	23.3	23.5	27.1
5.	Merchandise exports	17.4	19.4	16.3	16.2	19.4
6.	Services	6.3	7.3	7.1	7.3	7.7
7.	Repayments on U.S. Government loans	.5	.7	.5	1.0	.6
8.	Foreign long-term investment in the U.S.[c]	.5	.4	[d]	.5	.3
9.	Unrecorded transactions (errors and omissions)	.6	.7	.4	.8	—.9
10.	UNITED STATES PAYMENTS—TOTAL	28.9	30.5	30.0	31.6	32.7
11.	For imports of goods and services	19.8	20.9	21.1	23.6	23.3
12.	Merchandise imports	12.8	13.3	13.0	15.3	14.7
13.	Services (excluding military expenditures)	4.1	4.5	4.7	5.2	5.6
14.	U.S. military expenditures abroad	3.0	3.2	3.4	3.1	3.0
15.	Offshore procurement under military assistance programs	.5	.4	.2	.1	n.a.[e]
16.	Other military expenditures	2.4	2.7	3.2	3.0	n.a.
17.	Unilateral transfers	5.0	4.8	4.6	4.4	4.2
18.	Private remittances	.5	.5	.5	.6	.6
19.	Government transfers	4.4	4.2	4.1	3.8	3.6
20.	Military grants of goods and services	2.6	2.4	2.3	2.0	1.7[b]
21.	Other grants	1.7	1.6	1.6	1.6	1.7
22.	Pensions and other transfers	.1	.2	.2	.2	.2
23.	Private capital outflow	3.0	3.2	2.8	2.3	3.5
24.	Government capital outflow	1.1	1.6	1.5	1.4[f]	1.7
25.	DEFICIT (—) OR SURPLUS (+)	—1.0	+.5	—3.5	—3.8[f]	—3.8
26.	Met by gold outflow (—)	.3	.8	—2.3	— .7	—1.7
27.	Met by increased liquid dollar liabilities (—)	—1.3	—.3	—1.2	—3.1	—2.1

SOURCES: Department of Commerce, Office of Business Economics, *Survey of Current Business*, November 1959, June and December 1960, March 1961.

[a] Because of rounding to nearest $100 million, lines may not add exactly to totals and subtotals.
[b] Estimated at ⅓ of rate for first ¾ of 1960.
[c] Excludes investment in U.S. Government securities, which are included in line 27.
[d] Less than $50 million.
[e] Not available. Reported to be $130 million during fiscal year ended June 30, 1960. (*Survey of Current Business*, December 1960, p. 20.)
[f] Excludes $1.375 billion for increase in U.S. subscription to the International Monetary Fund.

enlarged (or the surplus reduced). Similarly, if aid is made available but its immediate effect is only to increase the foreign exchange reserves of the aid-receiving nations, it will not produce an equivalent expansion of American exports *during the period in question,* and will in this case, too, have the effect of increasing the United States deficit or reducing the surplus. If the aid is made available but spent for the goods and services of third countries, the effect on the United States balance will depend on whether those countries do or do not step up their purchases from the United States or their investments in the United States, and thus swell our receipts from abroad. If all of our foreign aid were translated directly and promptly into additional American exports, then neither total elimination of the program nor doubling its size would affect significantly our net surplus or deficit.

In a full-employment economy, an increase in government-financed exports could divert resources from the production of commercial exports that would otherwise earn foreign exchange. At the same time, American price levels would be subjected to additional pressures which might make commercial exports harder to sell. When, as at present, the economic resources of the United States are not fully employed, foreign aid programs can be expanded substantially, with no diminution in commercial exports or in domestic consumption and investment. The additional purchasing power, however, might increase domestic demand for imported goods. Under conditions of either full employment or less than full employment, exported goods are likely to contain some imported materials, albeit a smaller quantity in the case of the United States than for most other industrialized countries. All in all, it is nevertheless fair to say that foreign aid funds used for the purchase of American products have but little immediate effect on the net surplus or deficit in the balance of payments.

Not all funds under either the military or the economic assistance programs have been so used. The portions devoted to offshore procurement may have a bearing on the net surplus or deficit in the American balance of payments.

Offshore procurement under the military assistance program means using military assistance appropriations to purchase in one friendly country equipment which is then transferred on a grant basis to the country from which it was purchased or to another friendly country. Procedurally, it involves an "import" of equipment by the United States from the producing country and an "export" of that same equipment to its ultimate destination. The import is accounted for as though it were an ordinary purchase, and the export is accounted for in the same way as other transfers of military equipment. In the regular accounts, therefore, the item shows up three times, twice as a debit (once as a payment for an import and once as a unilateral transfer of military aid funds), but only once as a credit (i.e., as a receipt from exports of military goods and services). In balance-of-payments statements that exclude military transfers, the item shows up only as a debit—a payment for imports.[5] The dollars paid by the United States to the producing country may or may not be used to purchase American exports. If they are promptly used for this purpose, the effect of offshore procurement on the net surplus or deficit in the American balance of payments will be nil.

In relation to total United States payments abroad, which ranged from $17 billion in 1948 to more than $30 billion per year in 1957-60 (inclusive of grants of military supplies and services), military offshore procurement has never been a big item. It reached a peak of $640 million in 1955 and has been declining ever since—to $212 million in 1958, about $150 million in 1959, and $130 million during the year ended June 30, 1960. Thus, the only part of the military aid program which can affect directly the net balance of payments was shrinking rapidly at the time that the over-all deficit reached its postwar peaks. It should be noted, however, that the United States makes numerous defense expenditures abroad which are not considered part of our foreign aid program but which together pro-

[5] One of the reasons for the frequent exclusion of military transfers from the balance-of-payments accounts is a belief that they have no real impact on the international flow of trade, services, and monetary claims and that the items would not otherwise have been bought. The planes, tanks, and war materiel, it is alleged, do not serve to maintain consumption standards, to provide resources for investment, or to enlarge the production base of the receiving country. They represent a real resource, however, and it does not seem to this writer self-evident that their transfer has no impact on the flow of trade, services, and monetary claims.

vide friendly foreign countries with dollar earnings in substantial volume.[6]

One cannot tell from the balance-of-payments statement what portion of our economic aid has taken the form of exports of domestically produced commodities, but the information can be derived from other sources. Surplus agricultural commodities exported under Public Law 480 are, by definition, of domestic origin. The tied loans of the Export-Import Bank are fully counterbalanced by corresponding exports of United States goods. Since October 1959, this has been increasingly true for loans made by the Development Loan Fund.

The International Cooperation Administration, on the other hand, was able, until November 1960, to finance the procurement of supplies anywhere in the free world. It has reported periodically on commodity procurement expenditures outside the United States. Such offshore procurement averaged about $300 million per year during the fiscal years 1953-55 and slightly over $500 million per year during the fiscal years 1958 and 1959.[7] The increase could indicate a worsening of the competitive position of United States exports in world markets, an explanation frequently advanced as a significant factor in our total balance-of-payments deficit. It could also be explained, however, by changes in the composition of the aid programs, for example, increased purchases of items that have never been, or no longer are, produced in the United States.

The increase in offshore procurement under nonmilitary pro-

[6] Such expenditures include the out-of-pocket disbursements of United States military personnel and their dependents, direct payments to the foreign personnel employed by the United States defense establishment, foreign outlays of post exchanges and service clubs, payments to foreign contractors, foreign outlays of United States firms under contract with the Department of Defense, and direct purchases of foreign goods and services by the military agencies in construction programs abroad. For the past several years, defense purchases abroad (inclusive of offshore procurement under military assistance programs—lines 14 to 16 of Table I) have averaged more than $3 billion per year. They are scheduled to decrease substantially as a result of the directive issued by President Eisenhower on Nov. 16, 1960, and the policy statement made by President Kennedy on Feb. 1, 1961.

[7] Department of State, *Report to Congress on the Mutual Security Program for the First Half of Fiscal Year 1960* (General Foreign Policy Series 149), p. 61.

grams has been more than offset by the previously mentioned decreases in offshore procurement under the military assistance programs. While the over-all deficit in the United States balance of payments increased substantially, the direct effects of foreign aid expenditures on the net balance-of-payments position changed but little from 1953-55 to 1958-59 and are destined to decrease in 1961.[8]

Longer-Run Effects

So far we have been discussing only the direct effects of foreign aid expenditures, as reflected in the United States balance-of-payments accounts during the period in which the expenditures are made. The outflows of one period may produce inflows at a later date. Loans repayable in dollars result in a reverse flow when interest payments and amortization of principal begin. Loans repayable in local currencies produce a reverse flow if and when the foreign currency account is made convertible and used to extinguish the debt. All reconstruction or development aid which is successful, including grant aid, will, in the long pull, enlarge the production base and export potential of the receiving countries. The enlarged production base may enable them to dispense with certain imports which they have previously obtained from the United States or other foreign countries. The increased export potential will improve their competitive position in world markets, not only vis-a-vis third countries, but in relation to the United States as well. The pattern of world trade and world production will continue to change as aid recipients become better able to pay their own way in world markets—as it would change in any event—and the changes will require adjustments in the United States economy.

At the end of World War II, it was widely feared that the pro-

[8] New instructions on the balance of payments of the United States issued by President Eisenhower on Nov. 16, 1960, require the Department of Defense to reduce foreign expenditures from funds appropriated "to the military services and for the military assistance program" by "a very substantial amount" and the International Cooperation Administration to reduce the amount of commodities now being purchased abroad with ICA funds "to the lowest possible figure." (Text of directive carried in *New York Times*, Nov. 17, 1960.) See also President Kennedy's message of Feb. 6, 1961, to the Congress on the United States balance of payments and gold (*New York Times*, Feb. 7, 1961).

ductive capacity and other economic resources of the world were so heavily concentrated in the United States that other nations would be confronted with a chronic dollar shortage, regularly tending to spend more dollars for purchases in the United States than they could earn in sales to the United States or in third markets. From the United States viewpoint, foreign aid supplied the dollars needed to finance our commercial surplus. The dramatic change in Western Europe from dollar shortage to dollar surplus is in part attributable to the role of the European Recovery Program in evolving a better-balanced pattern of world production. Because of their improved economic position, France, Germany, and Great Britain were able, in 1959, to prepay more than $400 million due on outstanding loans from the United States and consequently to relieve the strain on the American balance of payments at a critical time.

No such dramatic improvement has occurred in the economic position of the less developed countries. Their needs for net inflows of resources from abroad (i.e., the deficits in their program balances) continue to be great. Meanwhile, our commercial surplus is smaller than during the early postwar years. A surplus is highly desirable, however, if we are to continue to transfer resources to the less developed countries.

Effects on Balance of Payments of Aid-Receiving Countries

At the start of the Marshall Plan, the European participants could not earn enough from their exports of goods and services to pay for the imports they needed. The foreign exchange reserves on which they might normally draw had already been reduced to the danger point. American aid would therefore, it was said, "bridge the gap" in their balance of payments. The bridging process in such cases is not analogous to making good an overdrawn check at a neighborhood bank.

As Machlup has pointed out, the gap was a program deficit, and a program deficit in the balance of payments is not one which first "exists" and then "is dealt with." [9] It is a deficit that is projected

[9] Machlup, *op.cit.*, p. 58.

when there is a chance to finance it or a desire to show the need for external financing. If the financing is obtained, balance is achieved at the desired level. If the financing is not obtained, the balance is struck at a lower level and some needs remain unmet.

Grants

From the viewpoint of the receiver, especially one competent to manage its resources, a grant of gold or a fully convertible currency represents the most desirable contribution to a program deficit. The grant requires no reciprocal yielding of resources and can be used to acquire needed goods and services in the cheapest available markets. Commodity grants deprive the receiver of the market option but are otherwise comparable to currency grants; they constitute a net addition to the resources available to the receiving country. In the subsequent accounting balance, the value of a grant appears on the inflow side of the ledger of the recipient country as a receipt from unilateral transfers and on the outflow side as a payment for imports.

Except for gifts of military supplies and equipment, there is almost no such thing as a pure grant. To the extent that economic aid on a grant basis requires the receiving country to release strategic (or nonstrategic) materials that would otherwise be sold abroad, or to provide local currency to a traveling legislator who would otherwise have to exchange dollars, or to meet some of the regular expenses of the United States Government, the receiving country sacrifices foreign exchange. So long as this reverse grant is smaller than the original one, the aid-receiving country will enjoy a net inflow of resources from the transaction, which should help to close its program gap.

Loans

Intergovernmental loans usually carry a grace period of four or five years before amortization of principal begins. The theory underlying the grace period is that the project will not be earning income until after the aid-financed equipment is installed and has begun to function. Principal repayments should not be demanded until the debt-servicing capacity of the country has been improved.

During the period of grace, however, foreign exchange will be required to meet interest payments, if the loan is repayable in a currency other than that of the borrower; the amounts required will increase at the end of the grace period, when repayments of principal will also have to be made. The higher the interest rate and the shorter the duration of the loan, the heavier the annual burden on the resources of the borrowing nation.

At present, loans that are repayable in inconvertible local currencies have an indefinite character. To the extent that the United States draws down the local currency account for miscellaneous United States uses within the borrowing country, repayment is being made in real resources. If the uses are ones for which the borrowing country would otherwise have earned foreign exchange, its balance-of-payments position may be slightly worse than otherwise. Often, however, the country would not have earned the exchange, because in the absence of the aid program the opportunity to earn it would not have been there. Local expenses of a traveling Congressman or of an American technical expert paid from the 10 per cent counterpart funds or from United States-owned local currency accounts deprive the foreign nation of dollar earnings only if the Congressman or the technical expert would have come to the country anyhow and exchanged an equivalent sum in dollars to cover his stay.

For loans repayable in local currencies, the chief balance-of-payments effects come if and when the bulk of the United States-owned local currency account is used to effect a transfer of real resources from borrower back to lender. Until there is such a transfer, the effect is about the same as that of a grant. Yet the very fact that they are called loans indicates either a genuine expectation somewhere within at least one of the parties to the agreement that repayment, in whole or in part, will become feasible at some future date, or it indicates the prolongation of a charade that no longer fools anyone of consequence.

The realism of expecting true repayment depends in large measure on the extent to which (a) economic growth occurs in the borrowing country without placing new strains on its balance of payments, and (b) such growth is accompanied by political responsibility. The rapidity of economic progress in the Federal Republic of Germany permitted the conversion of one billion dollars of prior grant aid into loan aid in 1953 and also permitted the principal repayments on its outstanding loans from the United States to be increased by $250 million in 1959. But the probability of similar miracles occurring here and there in Asia, Africa, and Latin America is not great.

Debt-Servicing Capacity

The capacity of the borrowing country to earn, through trade or other means, the currency of the lender (or currencies convertible into that of the lender) sets the limits on the amounts that can safely be borrowed. These limits are flexible, but are being approached in some of the less developed countries. Unlike the European countries, the underdeveloped countries by and large have not succeeded in building up their gold and dollar reserves since the end of World War II.

While numerous non-economic elements may seriously influence the *willingness* to service external debt from time to time, the *capacity* to do so ultimately rests on two economic factors. In the first place, the debtor country's economy must be able to do without an amount of domestic income and savings equivalent to the debt service. Secondly, the debtor country must be in a position to convert such segregated savings into the required foreign exchange. And if debt service is increasing, there must also be an increase in both the capacity to save and the capacity to transfer savings. . . .

In the short run, there may be a discrepancy between growth in income and growth in savings, and between the capacity to save and the capacity to transfer savings abroad. Despite slow growth in savings, income may grow fast for a time if the capital-output ratio is abnormally low or if the terms of trade are improving and the export sector is large in relation to total product. On the other hand, if inflationary fiscal and monetary policies are pursued, difficulties in the balance of payments are likely to emerge, despite a growth in income and savings. An inflationary situation results in an excessive pull of the domestic market for potential exports and particularly for imports. Thus the conditions necessary to assure a large or growing margin for debt service may be impaired notwithstanding a rise in income or even in savings. . . .

The analysis of change in debt-servicing capacity over time therefore requires an examination of the performance of debtor countries in both the field of income and savings and the field of foreign trade.[10]

In its published analyses of the external indebtedness of member governments, the staff of the International Bank does not treat loans repayable in local currency as external debt.[11] No additional outflow of foreign exchange from the borrower (or sacrifice of foreign exchange receipts that would have been earned) occurs until some or all of the local currency account is made convertible. At this point, the loan, in a technical sense, ceases to be a loan repayable in local currency.

What the borrowing country does incur is a contingent liability. Despite the exclusion of these contingent liabilities from some of the published data on external indebtedness, the staff of the International Bank is concerned by the marked growth in the debts repayable in foreign exchange of certain of the underdeveloped countries during the postwar period, particularly since 1955.

While European debt increased moderately between 1955 and 1958, the debt of non-European low-income countries rose by about 60 per cent. Asian, Middle Eastern, and African countries increased their debt by nearly 90 per cent, to a total of $4.9 billion in 1958. Latin American indebtedness rose by about 40 per cent, to $5.2 billion. Argentina, Brazil, and India each owed about $1.5 billion at the end of 1958.[12]

Among European capital importers, total service payments in 1958 required 2 to 5 per cent of external receipts, whereas among 32 countries of Asia, Africa, and Latin America, the ratio exceeded

---

[10] Dragoslav Avramovic, assisted by Ravi Gulhati, *Debt Servicing Capacity and Postwar Growth in International Indebtedness* (Johns Hopkins Press, 1958), pp. 57-59. Although it is true that balance-of-payments difficulties are likely to emerge "if inflationary fiscal and monetary policies are pursued," they may also arise in the absence of inflationary policies and despite a growth in both income and savings.

[11] Dragoslav Avramovic and Ravi Gulhati, *Debt Servicing Problems of Low-Income Countries, 1956-1958* (Johns Hopkins Press, 1960), p. 12.

[12] *Ibid.*, pp. 17-18.

5 per cent in 24 of them and it exceeded 15 per cent in the following twelve: Belgian Congo, Brazil, Chile, Colombia, Ecuador, Federation of Rhodesia and Nyasaland, Iran, Iraq, Mexico, Panama, Peru, and Venezuela.

In general, the ratios of private service payments to current account receipts are higher than the corresponding ratios on public account and are highest in the underdeveloped countries exporting petroleum and mineral products.[13] The service ratio on public debt, however, exceeded 5 per cent in 11 of the 32 countries, and 10 per cent in Brazil, Chile, and Colombia.[14]

From their surveys, the experts conclude that—

> . . . Despite the recent increase in international indebtedness of low-income countries—60 per cent between the end of 1955 and the end of 1958—the possibilities for further international lending are far from exhausted. There are a great number of countries which are still in a position to assume new long-run obligations. But in some cases uncertain export prospects and heavy debt service schedules constitute a serious obstacle to substantial amounts of further borrowing. Also, recent experience suggests that at certain points in the growth process, some countries incur substantial amounts of debt in a very short period of time; and this experience may well be repeated in other cases in the future. Hence, while capital exporting countries are showing a desire to accelerate substantially the flow of capital to low-income countries in order to promote their economic growth, they are also coming increasingly to recognize that not all of this financing can be provided on conventional loan terms. This has led to the creation of institutions (e.g., Development Loan Fund and International Development Association) designed to provide development finance on more flexible terms and in particular to avoid building up fixed debt service in foreign exchange beyond prudent limits.[15]

In this discussion it has been brought out that loans ultimately require an export of resources from the borrower in an amount

---

[13] In 1958, the ratio of total service payments (dividends and interest on private investment as well as service payments on public debt) to external receipts was 36 per cent in Iraq, 32 per cent in Iran, 25 per cent in Venezuela, 13 per cent in Ecuador and the Federation of Rhodesia and Nyasaland, 12 per cent in Chile and the Belgian Congo.

[14] *Ibid.*, Table XX, p. 72. A number of the figures are preliminary.

[15] *Ibid.*, p. 59.

equivalent to the sum of principal plus interest, if the loans are interest-bearing, or equivalent to the principal alone, if the loans are interest-free. Foreign credits consequently raise questions about the capacity of the borrower to expand its exports rapidly enough to earn the necessary foreign exchange. Grants, on the other hand, permit additional real resources to be imported without a subsequent export of real resources. The balance of payments of an aid-receiving country may also be affected in the same ways that the balances of third countries are affected—e.g., by opportunities to obtain contracts for offshore procurement and by the operations of surplus disposal programs.

Effects on Balance of Payments of Third Countries

The flow of grants and loans between giving and receiving countries can improve or worsen the balance of payments of third countries. The fact that offshore procurement provides such countries with a chance to improve their earnings from commodity exports (and, by inference, that "Buy American" restrictions deny them this chance) has already been noted.

American offshore procurement programs are now small in relation to American surplus disposal programs. The latter, it has been alleged, sometimes operate to reduce the export earnings of friendly countries, including countries that are receiving foreign aid.

At a 1958 meeting of the contracting parties to the General Agreement on Tariffs and Trade (GATT), for example, the delegate from Pakistan thanked the United States Government for the surpluses Pakistan had received and said that his country had benefited greatly from them. At the same time he pointed out that American shipments of cotton surpluses to other countries had resulted in lower foreign exchange earnings from Pakistan's cotton exports. He feared that the situation would get worse, observing that in the first quarter of 1958 as compared with the first quarter of 1957, Pakistan's foreign exchange earnings from cotton had dropped nearly 50 per cent.[16] Spokesmen for Greece and Turkey, nations that, like Pakistan, have received substantial assistance from the United States, have expressed both appreciation for the aid and bewilderment that our sales of tobacco under Public Law 480 might displace their country's normal marketings.

The sales, subsidies, grants, and barter arrangements of the United States are on the whole subject to the principle that they will not be allowed to disrupt normal trade, but the principle is difficult to adhere to in practice. Surplus disposal programs can harm third countries not only by displacing normal marketings of those countries, but also by preventing them from gaining a share of an expanding world trade in primary commodities. Canada and Australia, themselves generous dispensers of foreign aid, have been frequent critics of our wheat export programs.

At a GATT meeting in late 1957, the Canadian delegate pointed out that—

> his delegation did not object to . . . the extension of help to needy countries; indeed, within the limits of its capabilities Canada had also extended aid of this kind. Further, in more general terms his delegation had no objection to United States disposal programmes which had the effect of increasing consumption of the commodity in question by the amount of the disposal. The main objection was that, by a variety of techniques such as export subsidization, sales for local currencies, barter deals and tied-sales, the United States was promoting exports of wheat and flour with such determination and in such volume that it caused great damage to Canada's normal commercial marketing of these products. This was evidenced in export statistics from the United States and Canada in 1955-56 and 1956-57; while United States exports rose from 347 to 547 million bushels, in the same period Canada's exports fell from 309 to 261 million bushels.[17]

[16] Testimony of W. T. M. Beale, Deputy Assistant Secretary of State for Economic Affairs, in *International Food for Peace,* Hearings before Senate Committee on Foreign Relations, July 7, 1959, on S. 1711, 86 Cong. 1 sess., pp. 32-33. Some of the decline in Pakistan's export receipts may have been due to the fact that 1958 was a recession year.

[17] From an unpublished report of the remarks of the Canadian delegate at the meeting on Nov. 21, 1957, of the Contracting Parties to the General Agreement on Tariffs and Trade. This extract from the unpublished report is carried in *Wheat Surpluses and Their Impact on Canada-United States Relations,* by

The argument is valid not only for surplus disposal programs, but for any subsidized exports transferred in sufficient volume to affect world price levels and world output. Modernization of agriculture or industry in the country being assisted may reduce substantially its need for particular imports or increase markedly its outflow of particular exports—to the short-run detriment of certain other trading partners. Given the present distribution and composition of surplus commodity exports from the United States, it seems highly unlikely that the short-run losses suffered by other exporting nations are nearly as large as the gains enjoyed by the countries receiving the surpluses.

In the long run, aid which sucessfully promotes economic growth should, as a corollary, permanently expand the foreign trade of the country aided. The enlarged volume of world trade, with prospects for continued increases, should provide an environment in which virtually all trading nations will have a better chance to balance their international accounts at high levels, provided they have the flexibility to make necessary adjustments.

Recapitulation

Commercial exports and imports of goods and services are normally the major items in a country's balance-of-payments accounts. Transfers of commodities and funds from one nation to another via foreign aid also affect the accounts that register the inflows and outflows of payments. They affect them during the period of transfer and retransfer, both directly and indirectly. The new pattern of foreign trade and investment, which is then registered in the balance-of-payments accounts, modifies the pattern for later periods.

By definition, grants and loans under foreign aid programs of the United States Government are recorded on the outflow side of our accounts in the amounts extended and, by at least the portion thereof used to buy goods and services of American origin, on the inflow side as payments received for American exports. In an ac-

---

W. E. Hamilton and W. M. Drummond, Canadian-American Committee sponsored by National Planning Association (U.S.A.) and Private Planning Association of Canada (1959), p. 4.

counting sense, the effect on our net balance is small during any given year because most of the funds are used for goods made in America. The Department of Commerce has estimated that, of more than $5 billion in gross grants and credits extended by the United States Government in 1958, all but $300 million "consisted of equivalent transfers from the United States, mostly of merchandise and to a lesser extent of services, such as transportation and technical assistance."[18] The deficit, which has been a feature of the United States balance of payments during ten of the last eleven years and which increased so sharply in 1958-60, is not attributable to any significant extent to our foreign aid expenditures, which have been lower in total during those three years than in any other similar period of time since the close of World War II.

The tying of grants and loans to American exports helps to neutralize foreign aid as a factor in our international accounts. If all aid is tied, the Congress and the public can be reasonably sure that foreign aid programs will not reduce our reserves. Moreover, the domestic interests that benefit from the policy will be more likely to support the aid programs than if aid is untied. Conversely, exporters in other industrialized countries who gain from opportunities to earn untied American dollars may, if these opportunities are denied to them, exert pressure on their own governments for larger (tied) programs of foreign aid.

If all aid-giving nations adhere to the practice of tying their bilateral aid, each will be deprived of the opportunity to earn funds from the expenditures of others, to the detriment of its most efficient producers. Thus, the tying process is likely either to raise the total cost of aid programs over what they would be if purchases were made in the cheapest market, or to procure less aid for the same amount of money. In the receiving countries, tied aid inevitably complicates the business of matching requirements with availabilities. In the United States, tied aid is difficult to reconcile with our long-standing policy of promoting maximum competition in international markets.

In the receiving country, the value of a grant or loan appears

[18] Department of Commerce, *Foreign Grants and Credits by the United States Government,* December 1958 quarter, p. 3.

on the inflow side of its ledger as a receipt and on the outflow side as a payment for imports. Failure to obtain the resources needed to fill a projected program deficit for the coming year means a smaller inflow of grants and loans than had been hoped for and, consequently, a smaller outflow for imports. Unless the country possesses reserves that can be drawn down, it does not mean that an accounting deficit will have been registered at the end of the year, though it may mean that trade controls or stringent monetary and fiscal measures had to be introduced to prevent such a deficit from developing.

Aid that goes into the reserves of receiving countries rather than into the purchase of American products may temporarily worsen the United States balance-of-payments position. Such aid is not *ipso facto* unnecessary; larger reserves, particularly on the part of the less developed countries, are needed to support a growing volume of international trade.

The effects of foreign loans and grants on the market balance of payments, in contrast to the program balance and the accounting balance, have not been discussed. If a nation is suffering a persistent deficit in its market balance, the receipt of foreign loans and grants may only postpone the devaluation that will sooner or later have to take place.

If aid is obtained and takes the form of loans that really are loans and not euphemisms for grants, a retransfer of interest and principal must ultimately occur. This raises the question of the capacities of the aid-receiving countries to service foreign debt. Mention has been made of some of the factors affecting their debt-servicing capacity and attention has been directed to the fact that some countries have reached the point where debt service represents a fairly heavy claim on their foreign exchange earnings.

If and when the inflow of service payments to the United States exceeds the outflow of foreign grants and loans, the foreign aid program will have made a direct and positive contribution toward closing the deficit or increasing the surplus in our balance of payments. Persistent surpluses might create as many problems as persistent deficits. An important question, therefore, is whether it is possible, after an extended period of foreign lending during which new investment has exceeded the return flow of income and principal, to avoid the period during which the return flow exceeds the outflow and countries poorer than the United States might collectively be contributing resources to the United States.

The rate at which new foreign lending must grow in order for the inflows and outflows to remain in balance has been calculated by Evsey D. Domar.[19] This formula, in which it is assumed that amortization is a constant percentage of outstanding principal, shows that—

> if the gross outflow of new capital increases at a percentage rate equal to the average realized interest and dividend rate, a perpetual balance between imports and exports of goods and nonfinancial services will be approached. If it increases at a lower rate, an import surplus will develop. But if it increases at a higher rate, an export surplus will continue indefinitely.[20]

The formula is, of course, equally applicable to borrowers. If their inflow of capital from new loans can be made to increase at a percentage rate equal to the average interest and dividend rate being paid abroad by them, balance will be maintained. To exercise such continuing attraction for new foreign investment, however, economic growth in the borrowing nations would have to be both steady and promising.

[19] *Essays in the Theory of Economic Growth* (Oxford University Press, 1957), pp. 132-34.
[20] Walter S. Salant, "The Domestic Effects of Capital Export under the Point Four Program," *American Economic Review, Papers and Proceedings*, Vol. XL (May 1950), p. 506.

3

Types and Amounts of Aid

ACCORDING TO REPORTS compiled by the Department of Commerce, net foreign grants and credits extended by the United States Government between July 1, 1945, and December 31, 1960, amounted to about $75 billion. For the first ten and one half postwar years, the average was $5.1 billion per year. During the five-year period 1956-60, the average dropped to $4.2 billion. Both grants and loans have been available throughout the postwar period.

Major Foreign Aid Programs

The first major foreign aid program of the postwar era was administered by a relatively short-lived multilateral agency, the United Nations Relief and Rehabilitation Administration (UNRRA). Established in 1943, but most active between mid-1945 and mid-1947, it provided a broad range of relief and rehabilitation services on a grant basis to war-devastated allies on two continents, acting also as a claimant on their behalf before the Combined Food Board and other wartime allocating agencies. Thus, a few war-devastated nations that had sufficient foreign exchange were permitted to buy essential commodities through UNRRA. One of the recommendations adopted by the UNRRA Council at its first session was that "governments not in a position to pay make available to the Administration, in whole or in part, the local currency proceeds realized from the sale of supplies furnished by the Administration." [1]

---

[1] United Nations Relief and Rehabilitation Administration, *UNRRA—Organization, Aims, Progress* (1944), pp. 20-21.

Before a liquidation hastened by the growing tension in East-West relations, UNRRA spent the equivalent of $4 billion, 70 per cent of which was contributed by the United States. Of the 24 million tons of commodities supplied by UNRRA, about 90 per cent was shipped between July 1, 1945, and June 30, 1947.[2]

During the period of wartime planning for the postwar world, the hope of the United States Government had been that, after a brief period of grant aid, international balance would gradually be restored. For long-term reconstruction projects (as distinguished from rehabilitation projects financed by UNRRA) and for development projects, loans and guaranties would be available from the International Bank. Intergovernmental agreement to reduce trade barriers would expand the flow of private trade and private investment. Currency convertibility would become a possibility within the course of about five years. Nations finding themselves in temporary balance-of-payments difficulties would be able to draw on the International Monetary Fund, which, like the International Bank, was an outgrowth of the Bretton Woods Conference of 1944.

The true dimensions of the postwar reconstruction job were woefully underestimated, however, and the emergency period refused to draw to an early close. The plight of western Europe, which, unlike southern and eastern Europe, had received little UNRRA aid, became desperate. Rebuilding the second most productive workshop in the world seemed to the United States to deserve top priority, but the complex problems of the underdeveloped countries could not be neglected. Their long-suffering peoples were at last beginning to find their voices and make themselves heard. The United States responded with a generous series of emergency measures, primarily bilateral in character.

Britain's foreign exchange reserves, replenished in 1946 by a $3.75 billion loan from the United States and a $1.25 billion loan from Canada, melted rapidly in a brief, premature effort to make the pound convertible. Aid amounting to more than $600 million was made available to the newly independent Philippines under the Philippine Rehabilitation Act of 1946. Before the close of that

[2] George Woodbridge, *UNRRA* (Columbia University Press, 1950), Vol. I, p. 508; Vol. III, p. 429.

year, the International Bank had under consideration applications from nine countries for more than $2.5 billion in dollar loans.

Early in 1947, the United Kingdom informed the United States that, because of the deterioration in its own position, Britain would have to stop aiding Greece. The Greek Government, engaged in a bitter fight with guerilla forces spurred on and supplied by the Soviet bloc, had until then been receiving military and economic assistance from Britain. Under the "Truman Doctrine," this burden was transferred to the United States. The Congress appropriated $300 million to provide military and civilian supplies to Greece and, at the same time, $100 million to assist neighboring Turkey, which was also under pressure from the Soviet Union.

The year 1947 saw, in addition to the Greek–Turkish Aid Program, the enactment of a Post–UNRRA Relief Program and an Interim Aid Program to provide additional grant assistance, on a bilateral basis, to Austria, China, France, Italy, and several other non-Communist countries. Moreover, the War Department's program for the prevention of disease and unrest in occupied areas was vastly expanded.

Marshall Plan

By far the most memorable economic event of the year occurred on June 5 when Secretary of State Marshall made the speech that launched the plan that bears his name. American aid, he said, should not be "on a piece-meal basis as various crises develop," but should "provide a cure rather than a mere palliative." He invited the countries of Europe to draft a plan for their own reconstruction and to take the initiative in estimating their needs. The emphasis on joint programming and on permanently repairing the damaged fabric of the European economy was new and electrifying. "Economic viability in Europe was to be restored, thereby ending the need for relief. . . . With the revision of occupation policy in Japan, which was soon to take place, the objective of economic viability extended throughout the world." [3]

The Marshall Plan, known formally as the European Recovery

[3] William Adams Brown, Jr., and Redvers Opie, *American Foreign Assistance* (The Brookings Institution, 1953), p. 127.

Program, began in 1948. It was essentially a grant program for the reconstruction of Western Europe. Its objective was achieved in less time and at lower cost than estimated, but the emergence of an aggressive Soviet Union as an atomic power while the Marshall Plan was still in its infancy produced drastic revisions in aid philosophy.

Mutual Security and Related Measures

For the next seven or eight years, top priority was given to the building of military alliances and military forces capable of meeting "the Soviet threat." Concurrently, the ever more apparent needs of the underdeveloped countries highlighted their requirement not only for grants and loans in the form of commodities and equipment, but also for grants and loans in the form of information and expertise. Although there were numerous small-scale precedents for technical assistance, the "bold new program" called for in Point Four of President Truman's inaugural address (January 1949) in effect marked another new approach and added another new dimension to the aid programs.

At about the same time that technical assistance became a "program," the first major postwar program of military aid was enacted. The primary purpose of the Mutual Defense Assistance Act, passed in October 1949, was to provide military aid in the form of equipment and training to the Western European nations that had recently joined the United States and Canada as signatories to the North Atlantic Treaty. Under this act such aid could also be made available to other nations, among them, Iran, Korea, the Philippines, and China.[4]

With the Communist invasion of South Korea, the lines between different types of foreign aid were deliberately blurred and "defense" became the umbrella for most forms of American aid. The Mutual Security Act of 1951 became the first of a series of annual measures covering, in a single act of Congress, the continuation on a world-wide basis of military aid, economic aid, and technical assistance.

[4] See Department of Commerce, Bureau of Foreign and Domestic Commerce, *Foreign Aid by the United States Government, 1940-1951* (1952), p. 7.

During the early 1950's, rising stocks of surplus agricultural commodities, accumulated under domestic price-support programs, became available as an additional form of foreign aid. Provisions were then inserted in the Mutual Security Act of 1954 and thereafter requiring that specified portions of the appropriations be used for the purchase of surplus agricultural commodities which could be sold abroad for foreign currencies. Far more important, however, was the passage of the Agricultural Trade Development and Assistance Act of 1954, better known as P.L. 480, Title I of which permits the sale of surplus commodities for local currencies and the lending or granting of the currencies for purposes of military and economic assistance.

The loan repayable in local currency was not unknown before 1954, but it acquired new respectability about that time. Grant aid, it was felt by the administration and the Congress, should not become a permanent feature of international economic assistance. In the Mutual Security Act of 1959 the antigrant feeling was translated into a legislative requirement for the fiscal year 1961. Section 503 (c) demanded of the President "a specific plan for each country receiving bilateral grant assistance in the categories of defense support or special assistance whereby, wherever practicable, such grant assistance shall be progressively reduced and terminated." [5]

Defense support has meant economic assistance from the mutual security appropriation to enable the recipient country to maintain agreed military strength without retrogressing economically and thus to provide a foundation of stability on which other elements of the program (technical cooperation, development loans, surplus commodity assistance) can build toward economic progress. Defense support goes to a dozen of the 42 countries linked to the United States by defense agreements, but principally at this time to Korea, Taiwan (Formosa), Pakistan, and Vietnam. With the exception of Spain, the countries receiving grants for defense support all lie along the periphery of China and the U.S.S.R.

Special assistance funds are analagous to defense support funds. They are available for countries to which the United States does not provide significant amounts of military assistance but in which,

[5] 73 Stat. 252.

nevertheless, the United States has objectives that cannot be obtained by relying entirely on technical cooperation and development loans. Bolivia, Tunisia, Jordan, Ethiopia, and the Sudan are examples of countries currently receiving special assistance. The United States share in certain regional and world-wide programs such as the malaria eradication campaign is also financed from special assistance funds. To the Congress, the three broad objectives of special assistance have been summarized as follows:

1. To develop or maintain economic stability in countries in which some U. S. support is essential to continued independence or identification with the free world, and to support economic growth where, for political and economic reasons, the use of the Development Loan Fund would be inappropriate.
2. To secure or maintain U. S. military facilities or other rights in a country or to deal with economic and other problems arising out of the existence of such facilities.
3. To initiate or accelerate programs in health and education which further U. S. policy objectives by their humanitarian nature and by contributing to economic improvement.[6]

Lending Agencies

In view of the desire to phase out grant aid for development, the sources of loan aid are assuming increased importance. The principal American lending agencies are the Development Loan Fund and the Export-Import Bank. Established under the Mutual Security Act of 1958, the DLF is an independent government corporation to provide investment capital on flexible terms to the less-developed economies. A principal feature of this flexibility is the authority to accept repayment in local currencies. The basic law of the DLF requires it to encourage private enterprise and to beware of financing projects that may have adverse effects on the United States economy.

The Export-Import Bank makes loans primarily to finance the export of United States capital goods and agricultural products. Loans can be provided to private industries, governments, banks,

---

[6] *Mutual Security Act of 1959*, Report of House Committee on Foreign Affairs on H.R. 7500, H. Rept. 440, 86 Cong. 1 sess., June 5, 1959, p. 34.

or other entities abroad. With one significant exception, loans are made in dollars and must be repaid in dollars. Since 1957, the Export-Import Bank has been authorized under the Cooley amendment to P.L. 480 to make loans to private enterprise from foreign currencies generated by the sale abroad of surplus agricultural products.[7] Either American or foreign firms may obtain the loans— American firms for almost any overseas operation that does not dampen the prospect for United States exports, and foreign firms for expanding overseas markets for United States agricultural products.

While the United States has become increasingly committed to aid for economic development in the form of loans, aid under the military assistance program continues, with minor exceptions, to be provided on a grant basis. The military aid program initiated in 1949 consists in reality of several independent programs. By far the largest in terms of expenditures of United States dollars has been the materiel assistance program, under which munitions and other military supplies and equipment have been made available on a grant basis to friendly countries. Complementary to the materiel assistance program are certain programs designed to facilitate the development and production of military equipment and supplies "with particular emphasis recently on the more complicated military hardware in the more highly industrialized countries. These programs, with various names at different times, are now largely concentrated under those of the Weapons Production Program and the Mutual Weapons Development Program."[8]

In the international climate of the latter half of the 1950's, the defense umbrella that had been raised over virtually the entire foreign aid program of the United States after the invasion of South Korea became increasingly inappropriate, especially as a cover and justification for aid to underdeveloped countries. Recently, therefore, the United States has allocated smaller sums to building up

[7] The authorization is carried on in Section 104(e) of the Agricultural Trade Development and Assistance Act of 1954, as amended.

[8] From a report by the Department of Defense, "Military Procurement and Production Assistance Under the Mutual Security Act," in Department of State, *The United States Economy and the Mutual Security Program*, April 1959, p. 40.

military establishments in the underdeveloped areas as defenses against Communist aggression and placed greater emphasis on economic stability and progress where they appear to be most needed.

New International Agencies

Concurrently, a number of factors have combined to bring about a resurgence of American support for multilateral efforts to promote development. The efficacy of bilateral aid as a cementer of alliances is increasingly questioned. Western Europe and Japan have re-emerged as potential capital exporters, with strengthened reserves, while substantial deficits are being incurred in the United States balance of payments. The nature of the revolutionary currents sweeping across Africa, Asia, and Latin America is better understood, and it has become clear that these currents will not soon subside. The duties of all of the rich countries vis-a-vis the poor countries are more frequently stressed.

With United States backing, therefore, four new international aid agencies have come into being, three of them within the United Nations framework, and none of them as yet liberally endowed. Oldest of the four is the International Finance Corporation, created in 1956 as an affiliate of the International Bank, to invest risk capital in private enterprises in underdeveloped countries without the governmental guaranty required in connection with loans made by the Bank. "Since prospective undertakings are assessed on their merits as commercial investments, the Corporation does not normally concern itself with whether a proposed project will in the long run contribute as much, more, or less to the growth of the host nation's economy than other possible projects." [9]

The United Nations Special Fund began in 1959 to provide "technical assistance in depth"—aid for longer-term, basic resource surveys and other preinvestment undertakings not financed by the older United Nations Expanded Technical Assistance Programme. The articles of agreement of a new global lending institution, the International Development Association, have recently been ap-

---

[9] Committee for International Economic Growth, "The Role of Public Lending Agencies in International Economic Growth," Fact Sheet No. 7 (revised), Mar. 1, 1959 (processed), p. 5.

proved. Legally an institution, the IDA appears in reality to be a fund administered by the World Bank, out of which loans can be made on terms more flexible than those of the World Bank. No loans from this fund had been made as of the end of 1960. Combining attributes of both the International Development Association and the World Bank, an Inter-American Development Bank was created in 1959 as an additional source of assistance for Western Hemisphere nations. One of its departments, like the World Bank and the Export-Import Bank, finances development projects on "conventional" banking terms; the other department, like the Development Loan Fund and the International Development Association, provides credit on more flexible terms.

The soft loan is thus becoming more and more important as an international financial mechanism. As of the end of 1960, however, no multilateral agency is authorized to offer capital assistance for economic development on a grant basis.[10] Moreover, the authority of American agencies to make grant aid available for development purposes is being curtailed. Yet economic development is becoming the principal objective of bilateral as well as multilateral programs, now that reconstruction has been completed and military aid to underdeveloped countries is being deemphasized.

The proliferation of relatively autonomous agencies from which technical and financial assistance can be secured has certain advantages. At the same time, it severely complicates the problem of coordination—of making it more likely that the numerous potential sources of aid actually provide the right amounts, in the right forms, at the right times.[11]

[10] The United Nations Children's Fund and the United Nations Special Fund occasionally include items of capital equipment in specific projects, and the new International Development Association is not prohibited by its articles of agreement from extending grant aid after its first five years in operation.

[11] A reversal of what seemed to be the trend at the end of 1960 has been proposed by President Kennedy. In his message of Mar. 22, 1961, to the Congress he recommends a new "unified administration and operation" of American foreign aid; long-term interest-free or low-interest development loans repayable in dollars as the "instrument of primary emphasis"; and continuation of grant aid "for the time being."

Some Expenditure Figures and How to Interpret Them

Through its major and minor programs, the United States Government during the 15½ years between July 1, 1945, and December 31, 1960, provided, as has already been noted, net foreign grants and credits valued at nearly $75 billion. (See Tables II and III at the end of this chapter.) Some explanations and qualifications of the figures are needed.

In the first place, the $75 billion total refers to aid *utilized*—grants utilized and credits utilized. *Utilized* foreign aid is generally measured in terms of goods delivered or shipped during the period in question, services rendered, or cash disbursed by the United States Government to or for the account of a foreign government or some other foreign entity. The conversion of goods and services into appropriate dollar figures presents some difficult problems, and the solutions chosen affect substantially the apparent volume of aid extended.

Net grants represent the difference between new grants made by the United States and reverse grants and returns received by the United States from abroad. The latter include the dollar equivalent of counterpart funds made available to the United States and dollar settlements to close out certain accounts. Gross grants of about $67 billion made during the postwar period exceed net grants by about $2 billion.

Net credits represent the difference between new loans and principal collections on outstanding loans. Repayments of principal have tripled since 1950 and serve as a substantial offset to new credits. Interest payments provide a further return to the United States but are excluded from the totals. Principal repayments amounting to nearly $7 billion since mid-1945 reduce the gross credit total from nearly $17 billion to a net of about $10 billion.[12]

[12] On several occasions, aid originally given in grant form has later been converted into credit form. The $10 billion outstanding in the form of new credits excludes $2 billion in long-term credits resulting from the conversion of prior grants into credits. Similarly, net grant aid totals $63 billion rather than $65 billion if allowance is made for prior grants converted into credits. Collections of interest and commissions on credits extended amounted to $2.7 billion as of June 30, 1960.

Net grants and credits combined amount to $75 billion but gross grants and credits to $84 billion. These data exclude the capital investments of the United States Government in the Inter-American Development Bank, the International Bank for Reconstruction and Development, the International Development Association, the International Finance Corporation, and the International Monetary Fund. Payments to these five institutions (totaling approximately $5 billion), commingled with the capital subscriptions of other member governments, add to the resources available for the promotion of economic growth and the preservation of economic stability but do not result in immediate equivalent aid to foreign countries. Including such payments in total United States grants and credits would therefore make it impossible to distribute the totals in full by regions and countries.

The totals also exclude some $2 to $3 billion in assistance which takes the form of claims or assets of the United States Government accumulated from the sales of agricultural commodities for foreign currencies. A substantial part of these American assets will in due course be used to provide grants and credits to the country that has purchased the surplus commodities or perhaps to other foreign countries. The amounts, however, are not incorporated into the foreign grant and credit data until the foreign currencies are actually expended for grants and loans. Meanwhile, the country has the commodities and therefore has been aided.

By failing to include such assistance and the capital investments in certain international institutions, the total of $75 billion in net foreign grants and credits understates by more than $7 billion what is frequently referred to as "the burden of foreign aid on the already heavily burdened American taxpayer." On the other hand, by including expenditures that would almost certainly have been made by the United States Government for military equipment and agricultural commodities even if there were no foreign aid program, it probably overstates the burden by $10 to $20 billion.

Evaluating Military Equipment

Part of the overstatement is due to the method of assigning dollar values to goods that have been owned by the Government for some time before they are used in a foreign aid program. This problem is discussed briefly in John H. Ohly's revealing annex to the Draper Committee report. Tanks, for example, may be purchased from the United States Army by the military assistance program, with military aid funds. The Army will then use the proceeds of these sales to procure more modern equipment for itself. This it would soon have had to do in any event. Ohly's guess, probably an informed one despite his disclaimers, is that "reimbursements from mutual security funds which have in turn been employed to modernize our own Armed Forces already [in mid-1959] exceed $10 billion, and perhaps exceed $15 billion." [13]

Until the Mutual Security Act of 1956, it was possible for the Army to charge the foreign aid program the full cost of the new modern replacements, even though the old tank or plane cost only half as much. Moreover, overpricing did not end with the amendments to the 1956 act. This does not mean that the recipient countries have in any sense been cheated; they received a grant of tanks and planes that they needed and wanted. But it does mean that the dollar figures on military grants and total aid may be much larger than they would have been if the military assistance program had been charged the original cost minus depreciation. By the same token, military aid may show up as a larger proportion of total aid than it otherwise would.

Dollar equivalents must also be calculated for rifles or other items completely excess to the mobilization requirements of the United States but valuable to the foreign nations receiving them as military assistance. Replacements for excess equipment not being required, no United States financing is needed apart from repair, rehabilitation, and delivery costs. Ohly estimates the value assigned to excess military equipment supplied to foreign allies as at least $1 billion by mid-1959.

Since Ohly's brief discussion of the problem, the Comptroller General of the United States has released a report to the Congress on the pricing of materiel delivered to the military assistance pro-

[13] John H. Ohly, "A Study of Certain Aspects of Foreign Aid," *Supplement to the Composite Report of the President's Committee to Study the United States Military Assistance Program: Annexes*, Vol. II, Aug. 17, 1959, Annex G, pp. 288-90.

gram.[14] It calls attention to numerous specific cases of alleged malpractices by the Army, Navy, and Air Force, but makes no attempt to estimate their net effect in dollar terms. The conclusion, summarized in the letter of transmittal, is that—

> The military departments have received improper reimbursements for deliveries of materiel to the military assistance program (MAP). These improper reimbursements resulted from charging MAP for materiel that should have been transferred without charge as excess stocks and from charging MAP higher prices for nonexcess equipment than is provided for by the Mutual Security Act. With respect to nonexcess equipment, (1) older types of equipment have frequently been transferred at original cost without reduction to reflect current condition and market value, (2) certain assemblies and spare parts have been transferred at replacement costs which were much higher than original acquisition costs, and (3) other items were transferred at incorrect prices because of weaknesses in the compilation or use of pricing information.[15]

Evaluating Agricultural Surpluses

Agricultural surpluses bought directly or indirectly from the Commodity Credit Corporation with mutual security funds constitute a category of civilian goods similar to the military goods purchased from the defense establishment with aid funds. For such agricultural commodities, the United States has already paid (or would soon be forced to pay) from CCC funds. What price should the mutual security program pay—the cost of acquisition to the CCC, or the much lower "world market price" used for sales under Title I of P.L. 480, or nothing at all? The practice of ICA is to finance their sale by private exporters, who purchase the commodities from the CCC or elsewhere, add a fee for their services, and resell the commodities to foreign importers or foreign governments. It is fairly obvious that most of the $1.8 billion in foreign aid funds expended pursuant to sections 550 and 402 of the Mutual Security Act of 1951,

[14] *Review of the Pricing of Materiel Delivered to the Military Assistance Program by the Military Departments,* Report to the Congress of the United States, February 1960.
[15] *Ibid.,* p. 1.

as amended, would have been spent by the CCC if there were no foreign aid program.

Similarly, the dollar figure representing the value, at CCC cost, of surplus commodities transferred abroad as grant aid under Title II of P.L. 480 substantially overstates the export market value of the commodities. Further overstatements of the "aid burden" may result from the use of official rates of exchange in converting into dollar equivalents grants and loans of local currency accumulated through sales of surplus agricultural commodities under Title I of P.L. 480. Disbursements of such currencies under loans and grants to foreign countries amounted to an estimated $1.3 billion by the end of 1960. Evaluating the dollar equivalent of the local currency loan or grant at the official exchange rate, when the free rate would require a much larger amount of local currency to obtain the same number of dollars, makes the aid total appear unduly large. Furthermore, the local currency loans and grants do not represent an additional financial "burden" attributable exclusively to American involvement in foreign aid, for the agricultural surpluses in question would almost certainly have been purchased by the United States Government anyhow, though one wonders how they would have been stored or disposed of had P.L. 480 never been enacted.

The volume of commodities made available to date for reconstruction, military preparedness, and economic development abroad remains unchanged—and very substantial—whether its dollar equivalent is recorded in the archives as $65 billion, $75 billion, or $85 billion. The place of grants and loans in the programs under which the commodities have been shipped and the distribution of shipments among major regions and countries have, of course, undergone some noteworthy changes.

Trends Revealed by the Figures

In 1959, net grants and credits for the first time fell below $4 billion. (See Table II.) The 25 per cent drop over 1958 was due primarily to the offsetting effect of exceptionally large principal collections. Without the $400 million in prepayments mentioned in Chapter 2, net grants and credits would have been just over $4 billion, or about 10 per cent below the total in 1958. In 1960, net grants and credits are estimated to have totalled $3.85 billion.

The gross and net figures obtained from the Department of Commerce have not been adjusted for changes in the price level. A constant dollar level of foreign aid in an era of rising prices means that a shrinking volume of real goods and services is being provided; a decreasing dollar level of foreign aid implies an even greater shrinkage in the volume of goods and services. Between 1949, when net foreign grants and credits totalled $5.7 billion, and 1959, when the total was $3.7 billion, the export price index of the United States rose by about 18 per cent. Thus, to have provided about the same real volume of aid in 1959 as in 1949 would have required the expenditure of approximately $6.7 billion instead of $3.7 billion.

The burden of foreign aid on the American economy—assuming that the transfer of surplus commodities and equipment is as burdensome as the transfer of scarcer resources—is indicated roughly by the ratio of foreign aid expenditures to gross national product. In 1946 and 1947, net foreign grants and credits amounted to 2.5 per cent of our gross national product. By 1950 the ratio had fallen below 2 per cent and by 1955 to 1 per cent. Standing at 0.8 per cent in 1959, the burden of foreign grants and credits on the American economy was less than one third of what it had been in 1946. Related to national income rather than to gross national product, the ratio of net grants and credits was not far from the 1 per cent of their incomes that the advanced countries have been urged in United Nations forums to devote to the economic development of the poorer countries. Economic assistance, however, amounted to less than half of the net assistance furnished by the United States in 1959.

The big postwar programs have been grant programs. Net grants represent more than 85 per cent of net grants and credits utilized since mid-1945 and gross grants represent nearly 80 per cent of gross grants and credits. In dollar terms, grant aid reached a peak of more than $6 billion (net) in 1953. By 1960 it had fallen to about $3.5 billion (net).

Because imported food, for example, can be sold to raise currency to pay the army, and military aid can be employed to release resources for the civilian economy, statistics purporting to distinguish military from economic assistance, on the basis of the appropriation account to which the aid-financed imports of the receiving country are charged, should not be taken too literally. On the other hand, they are not without significance.

Military supplies and equipment are furnished on a grant basis and, during the years 1955-60, accounted for 55 to 60 per cent of net grant aid for the world as a whole from the United States. Reverse grants and returns are small and, for all countries combined, the difference between gross grants and net grants is insignificant.

Whereas the figures on net grants reflect adequately the over-all trend with respect to grants-in-aid, the figures on net credits do not tell the whole story on lending. Credits were important in 1946-48 but, for the postwar period as a whole, net credits amount to less than 15 per cent of net grants and net credits combined. During the years 1954-56, the net credit total was negative because principal collections in those years exceeded disbursements.

As might be expected, principal collections on outstanding loans have been rising steadily, from about $300 million in 1950 and 1951 to an average of nearly $700 million per year in 1957-60. The extension of new credits has more than offset the rise in repayments, however. Gross new credits utilized fell below $400 million in 1954 but rose to $1 billion per year in 1957-60. The effect was to raise gross credits, as a per cent of gross grants and credits, from 7 per cent in 1954 to more than 21 per cent in 1958, 1959, and 1960.

Gross grants and credits include a bulky constant, military aid, which (as noted above) constitutes 55 to 60 per cent of all grant aid. The growing reliance on loan assistance to finance nonmilitary aid is better indicated by comparing new credits with new economic and technical aid. New credits now represent close to 40 per cent of new economic and technical aid. The latter, it will be recalled, includes defense support, special assistance, and emergency relief, as well as aid explicitly earmarked for developmental purposes.

Regional Data

On a net basis, Western Europe has received more than 60 per cent of all the aid extended by the United States and about 70 per cent of the military aid. During the past 10 years, Western Europe has repaid more than it has borrowed; from 1951 to 1960, inclusive, principal collections exceeded new loans by well over $1 billion. Grant aid, both military and nonmilitary (but particularly the latter), has been declining steadily since 1953.

Insofar as the Kremlin-dominated area of Europe is concerned, over 90 per cent of the net grants and credits were expended before 1948. From 1949 to 1956, inclusive, the total was negative. The modest amounts since then include loans to Poland and grants for relief supplies donated to the League of Red Cross Societies in 1957 for distribution in Hungary.[16]

Next to Western Europe, Asia, with net grants and credits of over $22 billion by the close of 1960, has been by far the largest receiver of United States aid. Moreover, nonmilitary aid to the region is still rising. The rather noticeable increase in the proportion of gross economic and technical aid which took the form of loans in 1951 and 1952 is due primarily to the Indian Wheat Loan, originally proposed to the Congress as a grant. New credits as a percentage of new nonmilitary aid to Asia, after dropping sharply in 1953, rose from 17 per cent in 1954 to about 30 per cent in 1959 and 1960.

Less than 4 per cent of the net grants and credits extended by the United States Government during the postwar period has gone to Latin America, although that region has been a major recipient of private foreign investment. Military grants account for less than 20 per cent of net grants and credits and less than 15 per cent of gross grants and credits. Nonmilitary grants have likewise been small; public assistance has, to a greater extent than in any other region, taken the form of loans. Principal repayments on outstanding Latin American loans have been running in excess of $100 million per year since 1955, and in 1959 and 1960 approximated $150 million.

[16] The expenditure accounts understate aid to Poland, which has been buying surplus commodities for Polish currency that is being held as a United States asset pending its disbursal in the form of grants and loans.

Principal collections from Latin America have been larger than United States Government aid to Africa, last of the great continents to awaken to the revolution of rising expectations. Aid to Africa, however, has been increasing in recent years. The totals of net grants to Africa during the postwar period, and of net grants and loans, are both lower than they would be were it not for one exceptional transaction: a reverse grant payment of $92 million from the Union of South Africa to the United States in 1947, in return for wartime aid.

Country Data

The breakdown of military aid figures which would show country recipients by years is still treated as classified information. Nevertheless, enough data have been released to show which nations have been the major recipients of military assistance.[17] France has been by far the largest receiver, having obtained materiel and services (e.g., training) valued at $4.4 billion by September 30, 1960. China/Taiwan, with $2.9 billion, is second and Italy, with $1.9 billion, is third. Turkey stands very close behind Italy.

Some of the largest recipients of military aid have also been the largest recipients of nonmilitary aid. For the postwar period as a whole, the nations that have received more than $2.5 billion in nonmilitary aid are, in descending order of magnitude: the United Kingdom, France, the Federal Republic of Germany, Italy, the Republic of Korea, and Japan. In each case, the figure includes massive reconstruction assistance and, in all but the Korean case, the bulk of the assistance was obtained during the first few years after the close of World War II.

Looking at the distribution of expenditures for economic and technical aid for the last five or six years only would show more clearly the shift from reconstruction to other forms of economic aid. Among the major recipients of nonmilitary aid during the period January 1, 1955, to September 30, 1960, Turkey is the only European

[17] See Department of Defense, ISA Comptroller, "Military Assistance Program, Value of Programs and Deliveries, FY 1950-1960, By Area & Country," Feb. 15, 1960 (processed); and Department of Commerce, *Foreign Grants and Credits by the United States Government,* December 1959 quarter, Table 2, pp. S-9 and S-10. See also subsequent quarters.

nation. Those receiving more than $500 million during the period in question were: Korea, Vietnam, Pakistan, Turkey, Taiwan, and India. Their receipts were, respectively, $1.7 billion, $1.2 billion, $617 million, $559 million, $546 million, and $519 million.

Agency Data

The major lending agency, it will be observed from Table III, has been the Export-Import Bank, with gross lending of $7 billion since mid-1945 and net lending of about $3 billion. Loans also have been made under the mutual security program and related legislation ever since the enactment of the Marshall Plan in 1948. Such loans amounted to about $2.8 billion (net) by the end of 1960. Only about 15 per cent of this latter amount represented actual expenditures from the capital available to the Development Loan Fund. (Commitments, of course, precede disbursements; DLF commitments by the close of 1960 totalled $1.8 billion, of which $1.4 billion represented formally signed agreements and guaranties.) [18]

Loan disbursements under P. L. 480, an even larger source of loans repayable in local currencies than the DLF, amounted to the equivalent of about $1 billion by the end of 1960. More indicative of recent trends is the extent to which the DLF and P. L. 480 replaced other American sources of foreign credits in 1959 and 1960. Of $1 billion in new United States credits utilized during the calendar year 1959, more than $400 million were the result of DLF and P. L. 480 loans, and the ratio in 1960 appears on the basis of preliminary figures to have been similar. (The DLF portion—representing dollar expenditures repayable in local currencies—resulted in increasing the real resources available to the borrowing nations. The P. L. 480 portion, however—representing the utilization of local currencies accumulated from the sale of previously delivered commodities—did not increase the real resources of the borrowing countries.) Of $12.6 billion outstanding in the form of long-term credits at the end of 1959, about $2 billion was subject to repayment in local currencies.[19]

[18] The Development Loan Fund, "Cumulative Status of Credit Authorizations as of December 31, 1960" (processed).
[19] Department of Commerce, *Survey of Current Business,* May 1960, p. 23.

Aid Receipts and Income Levels

The available statistics reveal little about the principles, if any, which have governed the distribution of grants and credits to free world countries. Virtually every nation and every territory has received some assistance, but there is no readily recognizable correlation between the amount obtained and population, area, per capita income, or development potentialities. Given the changing and multiple objectives of United States Government aid programs, no such correlation could reasonably be expected.

Some of the richest countries have received the largest grants and credits, but there was never any policy decision that assistance would be distributed in inverse ratio to per capita income. That paradoxical result—to the extent that it is a result—is due chiefly to decisions having little to do with per capita income, namely, the promptness and strength of the American commitment to aid in the reconstruction of nations devastated by World War II and to the special place of NATO in mutual security planning.

Countries having military pacts with the United States have received not only more military supplies and equipment but also more nonmilitary aid than countries without such pacts. This is consistent with a frequently stated objective of economic aid: to enable the receiving country to support a larger defense establishment than it could normally support.

The influence of defense considerations on the distribution of economic aid from the United States tends to destroy any correlation, direct or inverse, that one might otherwise find between economic aid receipts and per capita income. Economic aid available from sources other than the United States Government is said to be taken into account in the distribution of American aid. If the United Nations figures on international economic aid per capita to selected underdeveloped countries during the five fiscal years 1954-58 are reliable, the variations, even among countries of similar per capita income levels, are enormous. Among 16 countries in which annual income is less than $100 per capita, aid received per inhabitant from American and non-American sources during the five-year period ranged from less than $1 in Indonesia, Saudi Arabia,

Sudan, and Yemen to more than $60 in Jordan and Korea. In India, receipts were $1.3 per capita, in Nepal $2.6, and in Pakistan, $6.0.[20]

Among 18 countries with per capita incomes between $100 and $200, Libya's aid receipts over the five-year period amounted to more than $100 per capita, Taiwan's to nearly $50, Guatemala's and Iran's to more than $20, and Ghana's to $2.3. Among 10 countries having per capita incomes in excess of $200, international economic aid per inhabitant during the fiscal years 1954-58 varied equally widely. Israel's receipts came to $115 per capita, Costa Rica's to $30, Lebanon's and Panama's to $18, Cuba's to $2.8.[21]

The promotion of a steady rate of increase in per capita output within countries, or of uniform rates of progress among similarly situated countries, has not been one of the stated objectives of international aid programs and has not been achieved. The United Nations has assembled index numbers of per capita product at constant prices for 55 countries, developed and underdeveloped. In the six Communist countries for which figures are given, the index rose by 19 to 35 per cent between 1953 and 1958 (or the latest year for which data were available). In the 49 free-world countries, per capita product in 1958 (a recession year) was higher than in 1953 in all but Canada, Chile, Morocco, Pakistan, Peru, and the United States. In 15 other free-world areas, including Ceylon, India, Thailand, Turkey, and the United Kingdom, the increase was under 10 per cent. Burma and the United Arab Republic, small beneficiaries of outside economic aid, registered a 12 or 13 per cent gain, as did Brazil, a somewhat larger beneficiary, and Taiwan, a major beneficiary. In contrast to Turkey's small gain, neighboring Greece registered a 30 per cent increase. Israel, the largest recipient of external aid on a per capita basis, registered the most spectacular gain in gross national product per person, an increase of more than 50 per cent.[22]

---

[20] United Nations, *Statistical Yearbook*, 1959, p. 428.
[21] *Ibid.*
[22] *Ibid.*, p. 449. Included by the United Nations is a warning that "the figures should be interpreted with caution. The per capita estimates are subject to considerable error and are appropriate for indicating general trends rather than precise year-to-year changes. The methods used to measure the estimates in constant prices differ widely; inter-country comparisons should,

Project and Nonproject Aid

The literature on foreign assistance is studded with references to programs, but only one of the numerous American and international agencies—the International Cooperation Administration—claims to be program-oriented. For the most part, foreign grants and credits are provided for specific projects. Projects may or may not be combined and integrated into programs.

The project approach represents an extension into the international field of terminology that became popular domestically more than a quarter of a century ago, when the United States Government undertook to provide work relief for the jobless. In present-day international finance, projects are the basic units to which funds are allocated by the International Bank, the International Finance Corporation, the United Nations Special Fund, the Export-Import Bank, and other agencies. The attempt to direct resources to specific, carefully defined undertakings is in large part a reaction from the disastrous experience of the 1920's, when international loans were made at high rates of interest for broad, ill-defined purposes, and followed by wholesale defaults. More productive use of resources transferred during the postwar period, it was believed, would be obtained if funds were tied to the financing of specific power plants, railroad improvements, and other undertakings. This would permit more accurate appraisal of amounts needed, goods and services for which the sums would be expended, arrangements for management, and economic and social benefits of the proposed undertakings.

The articles of agreement of the International Bank consequently limit loans to specific projects except in unusual circumstances. Neither the term "project" nor the term "program" appears in the language of the authorizing statute of the Development Loan Fund, but legislative history makes it clear that the terms cannot be ignored. The following colloquy took place in May 1959 when

---

therefore, be made only with the necessary reservations." Estimates for several countries such as Cambodia, Laos, Vietnam, and Indonesia, not listed in the United Nations table, are given in the *Supplement to the Composite Report of the President's Committee to Study the United States Military Assistance Program: Annexes,* Vol. II, Aug. 17, 1959, Annex H, p. 337.

Mr. Staples of the General Accounting Office appeared before a subcommittee of the Committee on Appropriations of the House of Representatives:

MR. PASSMAN: Will you cite other instances [in which the DLF violated the specific project concept]?

MR. STAPLES: Two loans to India totaling $75 million. $40 million was for the procurement of steel to be used in the manufacture of railroad cars and bridges. $35 million was for road transport vehicles and parts and materials to modernize plants in the cement and jute industries.

MR. FORD: Will you give the dates of those?

MR. STAPLES: On June 24, 1958, both loan agreements were signed. . . . They were dollar loans, repayments to be made in local currency. . . . We have not placed emphasis on the dates. We have placed emphasis on the purposes for which the loans were made as not being consistent with the concept under which the Development Loan Fund was established.

MR. ANDREWS: What would be wrong with making a loan to India for $40 million to buy steel to build railroad cars with?

MR. STAPLES: Simply because the concept under which the Development Loan Fund was established and which they themselves represented to the Congress was that loans would be made only for specific development projects which were susceptible of careful planning and evaluation in connection with the application for these loans and not for broad general credit purposes. In other words, it is not consistent with the concept under which the Development Loan Fund was created.

MR. CONTE: What could be more specific than steel for the manufacture of railroad cars?

MR. STAPLES: Because it is not identified with a specific project.

MR. CONTE: That is a project, is it not?

MR. STAPLES: That is a general undertaking to improve their whole railroad system.

MR. CONTE: What do you want to know, how many cars they will build and for how many railroads?

MR. STAPLES: The concept was to develop specific undertakings such as plants and dams.

MR. ANDREWS: The other loan to India was $35 million for cement and jute plants?

MR. STAPLES: It was for road transport vehicles and parts and materials to modernize existing plants.

Mr. Passman: You are not dealing with the merits or demerits, but you are stating these loans were in violation of the concept represented to Congress?

Mr. Staples: That is right.[23]

Mr. Staples later turned out to be not quite so right and the General Accounting Office beat a none too graceful retreat before the close of the hearing. A GAO opinion included in the appendix to the hearings legally cleared the DLF. According to the letter of the Assistant Comptroller General transmitting and summarizing the opinion, however, the legislative history bearing on the terms "project" and "program" brings out two salient factors:

(1) Most of the legislative history deals with projects; and (2) the expressed intent of the executive branch was that loans would be primarily for individual projects but there would be loans for some types of programs for broader but specific sectors of a country's economy. On this second point there was indication of apprehension by the chairman of the Senate Foreign Relations Committee that, under the broad powers proposed in the authorizing legislation, loans for programs might become the rule rather than the exception and the representative of the executive branch stressed that the legislative history should clearly reflect its intent not to do that.[24]

A similar legislative history is being built for the new International Development Association (IDA). Assistant Secretary of the Treasury T. Graydon Upton, chief witness for the executive branch, informed the Senate Foreign Relations Committee that the lending terms of the IDA are flexible, "but the emphasis is put on specific projects. While it is not specifically stated that a loan may not be used for a deficit, the whole tenor of the negotiations and discussions was such that the greatest emphasis will be put on specific projects. . . ."[25]

The validity of the notion that loans (or grants) to carry out projects ensure a better use of resources than the same sums for

[23] *Mutual Security Appropriations for 1960 (and Related Agencies),* Hearings before House Committee on Appropriations, May 20, 1959, 86 Cong. 1 sess., pp. 207-08. See also p. 1097.

[24] *Ibid.,* p. 1715.

[25] *International Development Association,* Hearings before Senate Committee on Foreign Relations on S. 3074, Mar. 18, 1960, 86 Cong. 2 sess., p. 18.

the execution of programs will be examined at a later point. Capital-exporting nations obviously need devices for assuring themselves that the resources they supply will be used efficiently and for purposes of which they approve. Projects are one such device. With acceptance of the establishment of national development banks, training institutes, improved transportation, and similar activities as projects, the concept has been broadened considerably since 1946.

The ICA provides both "project assistance" and "nonproject assistance," the latter being the basket of commodities required to help meet the general import requirements of the areas being aided. In theory at least, ICA assistance is intended to finance that essential part of a country program that cannot be carried on with the resources otherwise available. The number of projects financed each year from the various ICA allotments (technical cooperation, defense support, special assistance, and other) totals several thousand. In dollar terms, however, nonproject aid always exceeds project aid. This is true not only for the program as a whole but for each region except Latin America, where project aid regularly exceeds nonproject aid.[26]

The annual country program books of the ICA, describing in considerable detail the situation in each country participating in the mutual security program, the resources available to that nation, and the uses to which project and nonproject assistance will be put, are the end-product of a complex exercise.[27] The purpose of the exercise is to support the administration's appropriation request to the Congress. It is essentially a unilateral effort, shaped to meet United States needs and stressing United States objectives in the foreign country. It provides the basis for an endless series of interdepartmental meetings in Washington before it is presented to the Congress.

> . . . Because of the uncertain future of the [foreign-aid] program, due to much unfavorable criticism at home and frequent organizational upheavals, as well as certain limitations placed on

[26] International Cooperation Administration, *Operations Report, Data as of December 31, 1959*, p. 47.
[27] For a summary of the program procedure for foreign economic aid, see H. Field Haviland, Jr., *et al.*, *The Formulation and Administration of United States Foreign Policy* (The Brookings Institution, 1960), App. D, p. 178.

the program, especially the annual appropriation process, little encouragement can be given to the field staff to plan boldly, comprehensively, or in long-range terms. . . .

The machinery in Washington is bedeviled by all of these difficulties, plus others. A complex programing procedure has been developed, under the general guidance of the Under Secretary of State for Economic Affairs and the more immediate supervision of the International Cooperation Administration, in an effort to encourage more effective planning along the lines suggested above, but this is greatly frustrated by the proliferation of separate agencies, with their different purposes, legislative mandates, personnel, and policy approaches. While the International Cooperation Administration strives through interdepartmental meetings to obtain commitments from the various related agencies regarding their contributions to the development of particular countries, other agencies, such as the Development Loan Fund and the Export-Import Bank, find it difficult, for one reason or another, to undertake such commitments until a particular situation reaches such crisis proportions that they are compelled to act in concert.[28]

Much of the text of the country program books is classified. The relationship between the actual level of the United States aid program and the statement of the problems and requirements of the foreign country is tenuous. The whole exercise, useful though it may be in clarifying official thinking within the United States Government, is not designed to produce long-term development programs of the kind that are increasingly believed to be necessary and desirable for underdeveloped countries.

[28] *Ibid.*, pp. 65-66.

TABLE II. *United States Government Foreign Grants and Credits, Military and Economic, July 1, 1945—December 31, 1960, by Major Regions and by Calendar Years*

(In millions of U.S. dollars or equivalents)[a]

Area	7/1/45–12/31/45	1946	1947	1948	1949	1950	1951	1952	1953	1954	1955	1956	1957	1958	1959	Total through 1959	1960 (Est.)	Total through 1960 (Est.)
All Areas																		
1. Net grants and credits utilized [b]	2,010	5,473	5,768	5,415	5,651	4,155	4,637	5,043	6,344	4,982	4,505	4,353	4,459	4,564	3,676	71,034	3,850	74,900
2. Gross (new) grants and gross (new) credits	2,172	5,678	6,311	6,005	6,135	4,641	5,086	5,620	6,991	5,556	5,076	4,934	5,173	5,168	4,719	79,262	4,500	83,775
3. Gross (new) grants [c]	2,063	3,023	2,222	4,469	5,440	4,187	4,658	4,795	6,279	5,169	4,655	4,444	4,176	4,050	3,721	63,349	3,550	66,900
4. Less: reverse grants and returns	113	124	239	131	243	157	140	151	166	73	69	75	79	72	51	1,883	50	1,925
5. Military supplies and services	0	0	0	0	0	0	4	16	66	8	9	16	12	11	21	294	10	300
6. Economic and technical	113	124	239	65	243	153	123	85	103	65	60	59	67	61	30	1,588	40	1,625
7. Net grants	1,950	2,898	1,983	4,337	5,197	4,029	4,518	4,643	6,113	5,096	4,586	4,368	4,097	3,978	3,670	61,466	3,500	64,975
8. Military supplies and services	610	69	97	474	213	524	1,478	2,663	4,268	3,434	2,672	2,633	2,487	2,362	2,046	26,031	1,900	27,925
9. Economic and technical	1,340	2,830	1,887	3,864	4,983	3,506	3,040	1,980	1,845	1,661	1,914	1,736	1,610	1,616	1,623	35,435	1,600	37,050
10. Gross (new) credits [c,d]	109	2,655	4,089	1,536	695	454	428	825	712	387	421	489	997	1,118	998	15,913	950	16,875
11. Less: principal collections	49	80	305	458	240	329	310	425	480	501	503	506	635	532	993	6,345	600	6,950
12. Net credits [d]	60	2,575	3,784	1,078	455	125	118	400	232	−114	−82	−16	362	586	6	9,568	350	9,925
13. Net grants as percentage of net grants and credits	97.0	53.0	34.4	80.1	92.0	97.0	97.4	92.1	96.4	102.3	101.8	100.4	91.9	87.2	99.8	86.5	90.9	86.7
14. Gross (new) credits as percentage of gross (new) grants and gross (new) credits	5.0	46.8	64.8	25.6	11.3	9.8	8.4	14.7	10.2	7.0	8.3	10.0	19.3	21.6	21.1	20.1	21.1	20.1
15. Gross (new) credit as percentage of gross (new) economic and technical aid [e]	7.0	47.3	65.8	28.1	11.7	9.8	11.9	28.5	26.8	18.3	17.6	21.4	37.3	40.0	37.6	30.1	36.7	30.4
Western Europe [f]																		
1. Net grants and credits utilized	842	3,468	4,504	4,213	4,513	3,266	3,385	3,750	4,399	3,100	2,386	2,202	2,029	1,669	1,029	44,757	1,190	45,950
2. Gross (new) grants and gross (new) credits	976	3,593	4,757	4,404	4,851	3,599	3,744	4,235	4,838	3,497	2,691	2,554	2,317	1,979	1,771	49,808	1,480	51,290
3. Gross (new) grants	926	1,480	987	3,159	4,350	3,372	3,629	3,774	4,661	3,393	2,618	2,462	1,949	1,743	1,610	40,115	1,270	41,385
4. Less: reverse grants and returns	111	81	143	53	223	143	122	143	101	64	54	67	71	65	34	1,475	30	1,505
5. Military supplies and services	0	0	0	0	0	4	15	65	6	4	5	10	9	9	6	133	7	140
6. Economic and technical aid	111	81	143	53	223	139	107	78	95	60	49	57	62	56	28	1,342	23	1,365
7. Net grants	815	1,399	844	3,106	4,127	3,227	3,507	3,631	4,559	3,330	2,564	2,396	1,879	1,677	1,575	38,638	1,240	39,880
8. Military supplies and services	0	0	43	250	171	447	1,082	2,183	3,433	2,329	1,758	1,906	1,574	1,368	1,280	17,825	1,030	18,855
9. Economic and technical aid	815	1,399	801	2,856	3,956	2,780	2,425	1,448	1,126	1,001	806	490	305	309	295	20,813	210	21,025
10. Gross (new) credits	50	2,113	3,770	1,245	501	227	115	461	177	104	73	92	368	236	161	9,693	210	9,905
11. Less: principal collections	23	44	110	137	114	189	239	341	338	334	251	285	219	244	706	3,574	260	3,835
12. Net credits	27	2,069	3,661	1,107	388	38	−122	119	−161	−230	−177	−194	150	−8	−546	6,119	−50	6,070

13. Net grants as percentage of net grants and credits	96.8	40.5	18.7	73.7	91.4	98.8	103.6	96.8	103.6	107.4	107.5	108.8	92.6	100.5	155.1	86.3	104.2	86.8
14. Gross (new) credits as percentage of gross (new) grants and gross (new) credits	5.1	58.8	79.2	28.3	10.3	6.3	3.1	10.9	3.6	3.0	2.7	3.6	15.9	11.9	9.1	19.5	14.2	19.3
15. Gross (new) credits as percentage of gross (new) economic and technical aid	5.1	58.8	80.0	30.0	10.7	7.2	4.3	23.2	12.7	8.9	7.9	14.4	50.1	39.3	35.3	30.4	47.4	30.7

Other Europe g

1. Net grants and credits utilized	274	677	186	3	−24	−9	−15	−4	4	7	−1	−3	15	24	9	1,143	1	1,145
2. Gross (new) grants and gross (new) credits	274	679	186	19	1	*	0	0	8	11	4	3	18	28	16	1,247	12	1,260
3. Gross (new) grants	274	607	155	0	0	*	0	0	8	11	4	3	7	1	2	1,074	4	1,080
4. Less: reverse grants and returns	0	2	0	8	8	9	13	0	0	*	*	0	0	0	0	39	0	40
5. Military supplies and services	0	0	0	0	0	0	0	0	0	*	*	0	0	0	0	0	0	0
6. Economic and technical aid	0	2	0	8	8	9	13	0	0	*	*	0	0	0	0	39	0	40
7. Net grants	274	605	155	0	−8	−9	−13	0	8	11	4	3	7	1	2	1,034	4	1,040
8. Military supplies and services	0	0	0	0	0	0	0	0	0	0	0	0	0	0	0	0	0	0
9. Economic and technical aid	274	605	155	0	−8	−9	−13	0	8	11	4	3	7	1	2	1,034	4	1,040
10. Gross (new) credits	0	72	31	19	1	0	0	0	0	0	0	0	11	27	14	175	8	180
11. Less: principal collections	0	0	1	8	18	1	1	4	4	4	5	6	3	4	7	66	11	75
12. Net credits	0	72	30	11	−16	−1	−1	−4	−4	−4	−5	−6	8	23	7	109	−3	105
13. Net grants as percentage of net grants and credits	100.0	89.4	83.3	(k)	(k)	(k)	(k)	(k)	(k)	(k)	(k)	(k)	46.7	4.2	(k)	90.5	(k)	90.8
14. Gross (new) credits as percentage of gross (new) grants and gross (new) credits	0	10.6	16.7	100.0	(k)	0	0	0	0	0	0	0	61.1	96.4	87.5	14.0	66.7	14.3
15. Gross (new) credits as percentage of gross (new) economic and technical aid	0	10.6	16.7	100.0	(k)	0	0	0	0	0	0	0	61.1	96.4	87.5	14.0	66.7	14.3

Asia h

1. Net grants and credits utilized	803	944	956	1,042	967	725	999	1,003	1,411	1,619	1,845	1,838	1,872	2,110	1,924	20,057	2,125	22,180
2. Gross (new) grants and gross (new) credits	821	976	1,122	1,236	1,040	808	1,023	1,036	1,486	1,690	1,958	1,916	2,132	2,235	2,033	21,513	2,240	23,755
3. Gross (new) grants	788	629	923	1,175	956	688	858	838	1,402	1,579	1,782	1,658	1,835	1,930	1,044	18,686	1,780	20,465
4. Less: reverse grants and returns	2	20	3	70	12	5	3	8	8	8	14	8	9	5	17	194	15	210
5. Military supplies and services	0	0	0	67	0	0	1	1	1	3	3	5	3	2	15	102	5	110
6. Economic and technical aid	2	20	3	3	12	5	2	7	7	5	11	3	6	3	2	92	10	100
7. Net grants	786	609	919	1,105	943	685	855	830	1,395	1,570	1,768	1,650	1,827	1,923	1,628	18,491	1,765	20,255
8. Military supplies and services	610	69	54	224	42	63	291	383	769	1,037	862	643	814	885	671	7,417	780	8,200
9. Economic and technical aid	176	540	865	881	901	622	564	447	626	533	906	1,007	1,013	1,038	957	11,074	985	12,060
10. Gross (new) credits	33	347	199	61	84	121	165	198	84	111	176	258	297	305	389	2,826	465	3,290
11. Less: principal collections	17	12	163	123	61	80	20	24	67	62	100	69	253	118	93	1,261	105	1,365
12. Net credits	16	335	36	−63	22	41	144	174	17	48	75	190	43	187	296	1,564	360	1,925
13. Net grants as percentage of net grants and credits	97.9	64.5	96.1	106.0	97.5	94.5	85.6	82.8	98.9	97.0	95.8	89.9	97.6	91.1	84.6	92.2	83.1	91.3
14. Gross (new) credits as percentage of gross (new) grants and gross (new) credits	4.0	35.6	17.7	4.9	8.1	15.0	16.1	19.1	5.6	6.6	9.0	13.5	13.9	13.6	19.1	13.1	20.8	13.8
15. Gross (new) credits as percentage of gross (new) economic and technical aid	15.6	38.2	18.6	6.4	8.4	16.2	22.6	30.4	11.7	17.1	16.1	20.3	22.6	22.6	28.8	20.2	31.8	21.3

TABLE II. *United States Government Foreign Grants and Credits, Military and Economic, July 1, 1945—December 31, 1960, by Major Regions and by Calendar Years*—Continued

(In millions of U.S. dollars or equivalents)[a]

Area	7/1/45–12/31/45	1946	1947	1948	1949	1950	1951	1952	1953	1954	1955	1956	1957	1958	1959	Total through 1959	1960 (Est.)	Total through 1960 (Est.)
Africa [b]																		
1. Net grants and credits utilized	1	13	−87	−3	8	8	5	55	42	52	89	71	60	65	147	527	205	735
2. Gross (new) grants and gross (new) credits	1	13	6	5	9	9	7	56	52	61	100	84	86	91	174	755	230	990
3. Gross (new) grants	*	0	1	0	0	*	2	4	8	15	57	48	54	65	121	377	155	535
4. Less: reverse grants and returns	0	0	92	0	0	0	0	0	0	*	*	*	*	*	*	92	*	95
5. Military supplies and services	0	0	0	0	0	0	0	0	0	0	0	0	0	0	0	*	*	2
6. Economic and technical aid	0	0	92	0	0	*	0	0	0	0	0	0	0	0	0	92	0	92
7. Net grants	*	−*	−91	0	−*	*	2	4	8	15	57	48	54	65	120	283	155	440
8. Military supplies and services	0	0	0	0	0	0	0	0	2	2	3	2	9	9	7	34	10	45
9. Economic and technical aid	*	−*	−91	0	−*	*	2	4	6	13	54	46	45	56	113	250	145	395
10. Gross (new) credits	1	13	5	5	9	9	5	52	44	46	43	36	32	26	53	380	75	455
11. Less: principal collections	−*	−*	1	9	1	1	2	2	10	8	10	15	26	26	25	137	25	160
12. Net credits	1	13	4	−3	8	8	4	50	34	38	33	22	6	−*	28	243	50	295
13. Net grants as percentage of net grants and credits	(k)	(k)	(k)	0	(k)	(k)	(k)	7.3	19.0	28.8	64.0	67.6	90.0	100.0	81.6	53.7	75.6	59.9
14. Gross (new) credits as percentage of gross (new) grants and gross (new) credits	(k)	100.0	(k)	(k)	(k)	(k)	(k)	92.8	84.6	75.4	45.0	42.8	37.2	28.6	30.4	50.4	32.6	46.0
15. Gross (new) credits as percentage of gross (new) economic and technical aid	(k)	(k)	(k)	(k)	(k)	(k)	(k)	92.8	88.0	78.0	44.3	43.9	41.6	31.7	31.9	52.6	54.1	48.3
Latin America																		
1. Net grants and credits utilized	26	95	101	41	64	38	161	132	403	125	103	112	338	575	390	2,705	160	2,865
2. Gross (new) grants and gross (new) credits	35	120	132	80	108	95	208	184	513	204	227	227	466	708	546	3,856	325	4,180
3. Gross (new) grants	10	20	48	19	31	21	79	83	114	89	98	137	176	184	164	1,276	135	1,410
4. Less: reverse grants and returns	0	0	*	*	0	0	0	0	0	*	*	*	*	*	*	54	*	55
5. Military supplies and services	0	*	0	0	*	0	0	0	53	*	*	*	*	*	*	53	*	54
6. Economic and technical aid	0	*	0	*	0	0	0	0	0	*	*	0	*	*	*	1	*	1
7. Net grants	10	20	48	19	31	21	79	83	61	89	98	137	176	184	164	1,221	135	1,355
8. Military supplies and services	0	0	0	0	0	0	64	60	34	47	30	56	66	71	59	488	40	525
9. Economic and technical aid	10	20	48	19	31	21	15	23	27	42	68	81	110	113	105	733	95	830

10. Gross (new) credits	25	100	84	61	77	74	129	101	399	115	129	90	290	524	382	2,580	190	2,770
11. Less: principal collections	9	25	31	40	44	57	47	52	57	79	124	116	128	133	156	1,097	165	1,260
12. Net credits	16	75	53	22	34	17	81	49	343	36	5	−25	162	391	226	1,485	25	1,510
13. *Net grants as percentage of net grants and credits*	*38.5*	*81.0*	*47.5*	*46.3*	*48.4*	*55.3*	*49.1*	*68.9*	*15.1*	*71.2*	*95.1*	*122.3*	*52.1*	*32.0*	*42.0*	*45.1*	*84.4*	*47.3*
14. *Gross (new) credits as percentage of gross (new) grants and gross (new) credits*	*71.4*	*83.3*	*63.6*	*76.2*	*71.3*	*77.9*	*68.0*	*54.9*	*77.8*	*56.4*	*56.8*	*39.6*	*62.2*	*74.0*	*70.0*	*66.9*	*58.5*	*66.3*
15. *Gross (new) credits as percentage of gross (new) economic and technical aid*	*71.4*	*83.3*	*63.6*	*76.2*	*71.3*	*77.9*	*89.6*	*81.4*	*93.7*	*73.2*	*65.5*	*62.6*	*72.5*	*82.5*	*78.4*	*77.8*	*66.7*	*76.9*
Other[i]																		
1. Net grants and credits utilized	65	276	108	120	122	128	102	105	84	78	80	131	147	120	176	1,844	175	2,020
2. Gross (new) grants and gross (new) credits	65	296	108	261	125	130	103	107	91	93	95	146	154	127	181	2,082	190	2,270
3. Gross (new) grants	65	285	108	117	104	106	86	94	84	81	95	133	154	127	181	1,823	190	2,015
4. Less: reverse grants and returns	0	20	0	0	0	0	0	0	3	2	0	0	0	1	0	26	1	25
5. Military supplies and services	0	0	0	0	0	0	0	0	0	2	0	0	0	0	0	5	0	5
6. Economic and technical aid	0	20	0	0	0	0	0	0	3	0	0	0	0	1	0	21	1	20
7. Net grants	65	265	108	117	104	106	89	94	81	79	95	133	154	126	181	1,796	190	1,985
8. Military supplies and services	0	0	0	0	0	15	40	36	30	18	19	25	25	28	29	264	25	290
9. Economic and technical aid	65	265	108	117	104	91	49	58	51	61	76	108	129	98	152	1,532	165	1,695
10. Gross (new) credits	0	11	*	144	21	24	13	7	12	*	13	*	*	*	259	0	260
11. Less: principal collections	0	*	*	140	1	2	1	2	4	14	15	16	7	6	5	211	15	225
12. Net credits	0	11	0	4	19	22	13	11	3	−1	−15	−2	−7	−6	−5	49	−15	35

SOURCES: Records made available by the Department of Commerce, Office of Business Economics, Balance of Payments Division, for pre-1960 data. 1960 estimates by author, based on information for first three quarters in Department of Commerce, *Foreign Grants and Credits by the United States Government*, September 1960 quarter.

* = less than $500,000; −* = net minus of less than $500,000.

[a] Because of rounding, components may not add to totals. This is especially true with respect to the estimates in the last two columns. The totals do not include the capital investments ($4,949 million) of the U. S. Government in the Inter-American Development Bank ($80 million), the International Bank ($635 million), the International Development Association ($74 million), the International Finance Corporation ($35 million), and the International Monetary Fund ($4,125 million). Payments to these five institutions do not result in immediate equivalent aid to foreign countries. The totals also exclude assistance through the accumulation of foreign currency claims, as indicated on line 44 of Table III.

[b] Utilized grants and credits are measured generally in terms of goods delivered or shipped, services rendered, or cash disbursed by the U. S. Government to or for the account of a foreign government or other foreign entity.

[c] New credits do not include $2,257 million representing conversion of prior grants into credits as agreed in certain settlements for postwar relief and other grants. New grants have not been adjusted for any part of these settlements. The $2,257 million total is distributed as follows, in millions of dollars with years to which the conversion is applicable shown in parentheses: Western Europe: $1,969, of which $562 (1945), $353 (1946), $47 (1947), $7 (1948), $1,000 (1953); Other Europe: $222 (1945); Asia: $62, of which $9 (1945), $51 (1946), $2 (1948); Latin America: $3 of which $2 (1950), $1 (1956); Africa: less than $.5. Prior grants converted into credits amounting to $50 million in the case of China and $222 million in the case of the U.S.S.R. are so recorded by the Department of Commerce for statistical convenience; the settlements with these countries are still to be reached.

[d] Credits are to be regarded as nonmilitary aid only, since virtually all military aid takes the form of grants.

[e] i.e., line 10 as percentage of lines 6+9+10.

[f] Includes Greece, Turkey, and Yugoslavia. Because of the inclusion of certain dependencies of Western European countries with the mother countries, data for Western Europe are slightly overstated and data for other regions, particularly Asia and Africa, are correspondingly understated. A further overstatement of the Western European totals is due to the inclusion of some non-European military aid in the regional totals for Western Europe.

[g] "Other Europe" means U.S.S.R. and European Communist states other than Yugoslavia.

[h] Because of the inclusion of certain Asian and African dependencies in Western European totals, data for Asia and Africa are correspondingly understated.

[i] Includes Australia, Canada, New Zealand, some unspecified areas, and certain international organizations. Percentages for "Other" have not been computed because of the heterogeneous nature of the category.

[k] Percentage not meaningful, either because underlying figures are too small or negative.

TABLE III. *Summary of United States Government Foreign Grants and Credits, Military and Economic, July 1, 1945–December 31, 1960, by Type and Program* [a]

(In millions of U. S. dollars or equivalents)

	Type and Program	7/1/45–12/31/52	1953	1954	1955	1956	1957	1958	1959	Total through 1959	1960 (Est.)	Total through 1960 (Est.)
1.	NET TOTAL, AID PROGRAMS	38,152	6,344	4,982	4,505	4,353	4,459	4,564	3,676	71,034	3,850	74,900
	Grants											
2.	Net	29,558	6,113	5,096	4,586	4,368	4,097	3,978	3,670	61,466	3,500	64,975
3.	Gross (new) [b]	30,855	6,279	5,169	4,655	4,444	4,176	4,050	3,721	63,349	3,550	66,900
4.	Military supplies and services [c]	6,281	4,332	3,442	2,681	2,649	2,500	2,372	2,067	26,325	1,900	28,225
	Mutual security and related programs:											
5.	Military supplies and services	4,602	4,063	3,058	2,250	2,561	2,378	2,268	1,899	23,080	1,700	24,775
6.	Multilateral-construction program contributions	73	91	69	84	68	65	81	58	589	125	725
7.	Military equipment "loans"		47	69	53	20	57	23	110	379	75	450
8.	Chinese and Japanese military aid	120		246	294					660		660
9.	Lend-lease	679								679		680
10.	Greek-Turkish aid	530								530		530
11.	Chinese naval and Philippine military aid	273								273		275
12.	Military equipment "loans" (other than mutual security) [e]	4	131							135		135
13.	Other (economic and technical)	24,575	1,947	1,726	1,975	1,795	1,676	1,677	1,653	37,025	1,650	38,675
	Mutual security and related programs:											
14.	Commodity Credit Corporation stocks for famine and other urgent relief		68	56	78	109	61	77	57	507	75	575
15.	Foreign currencies under Agricultural Trade Development and Assistance Act					12	62	99	85	258	75	335
16.	Other (development assistance, technical assistance, and relief)	12,777	1,680	1,570	1,685	1,467	1,350	1,310	1,381	23,219	1,325	24,550
17.	Civilian supplies and lend-lease	6,890	139	39	8	1	(d)	2	2	7,082		7,080
18.	UNRRA, post-UNRRA, and interim aid	3,443								3,443		3,445
19.	Philippine rehabilitation	634	(d)	(d)						635		635
20.	Donations of agricultural surpluses	55	37	49	187	187	175	159	107	955	125	1,080
21.	Miscellaneous	776	23	12	17	19	28	30	21	926	50	975
22.	Less: Reverse grants and returns	1,298	166	73	69	75	79	72	51	1,883	50	1,925
23.	Military supplies and services	153	64	8	9	16	12	11	21	294	10	300
24.	Other (economic and technical)	1,144	103	65	60	59	67	61	30	1,588	40	1,625
	Credits											
25.	Net	8,594	232	–114	–82	–16	362	586	6	9,568	350	9,925
26.	Gross (new) [b]	10,790	712	387	421	489	997	1,118	998	15,913	950	16,875
27.	Under Export-Import Bank Act	3,415	647	276	207	229	667	646	493	6,582	400	6,985

	Under Mutual Security (and related) Acts:										
28.	Development Loan Fund									225	400
29.	Program loans	1,525		71	144		183		166	65	2,525
30.	Deficiency and basic materials development	85	28	23	11	177	(d)	230	2,462		150
	Under Agricultural Trade Development and Assistance Act:		26						147		
31.	Foreign government loans			48	48	60	146	234	709	240	950
32.	Private enterprise loans							2	22	20	40
33.	Lend-lease and surplus property	1,556	(d)			6			1,562		1,560
34.	British loan	3,750	11						3,750		3,750
35.	Other credits	459		17	10	15	1	(d)	513		515
36.	Less: Principal collections	2,196	480	501	503	506	635	532	6,345	600	6,950
37.	Under Export-Import Bank Act	1,125	311	346	308	262	318	314	3,591	370	3,970
	Under Mutual Security (and related) Acts:										
38.	Development Loan Fund	(d)	(d)	(d)	(d)				4	10	15
39.	Program loans	1	14	10	10	14	20	4	81	25	105
40.	Deficiency and basic materials development		97	78	118	10	15	24	96	15	110
41.	Lend-lease, surplus property, and grants converted into credits	382	46	47	48	157	269	16	1,491	120	1,600
42.	British loan	90	13	20	17	49		275	383	50	440
43.	Other credits	599				13	13	52	699	10	710
								15			
	Memorandum										
44.	Other assistance (through net accumulation of foreign currency claims)								2,245	525	2,775
45.	Farm product sales								5,073	1,150	6,225
46.	Under Mutual Security Acts								1,667	175	1,850
47.	Under Agricultural Trade Development and Assistance Act								3,374	975	4,350
48.	Under Commodity Credit Corporation Charter Act								32		25
49.	Less: Currencies disbursed for grants, credits, and other uses								2,828	625	3,450
50.	Under Mutual Security Acts								1,434	175	1,600
51.	For economic grants and credits to purchasing country								1,120	125	1,250
52.	Other (triangular trade and intercountry transfers)								314	50	350
53.	Under Agricultural Trade Development and Assistance Act								1,368	450	1,825
54.	For economic grants and credits to purchasing country								978	325	1,300
55.	Other (triangular trade and intercountry transfers)								389	125	525
56.	Under Commodity Credit Corporation Charter Act: other than for grants and credits								25		25

Sources: Records made available by the Department of Commerce, Office of Business Economics, Balance of Payments Division, for pre-1960 data. 1960 estimates by author based on information for first three quarters in Department of Commerce, Office of Business Economics, *Foreign Grants and Credits by the United States Government*, September 1960 Quarter, Table 1-B. Latter is also source of memorandum data.

[a] Because of rounding, components may not add to totals. The totals do not include the capital investments ($4,949 million) of the U.S. Government in the Inter-American Development Bank ($80 million), the International Bank ($635 million), the International Development Association ($74 million), the International Finance Corporation ($35 million), and the International Monetary Fund ($4,125 million).

[b] New credits do not include $2,257 million representing conversion of prior grants into credits as agreed in certain settlements for postwar relief and other grants. New grants have not been adjusted for any part of these settlements.

[c] Includes contributions to multilateral construction program of the North Atlantic Treaty Organization and contributions to mutual special weapons projects.

[d] Less than $500,000.

[e] These "loans" by the Defense Department are essentially transfers on an indeterminate basis, generally requiring only the return of the actual item, if available, as was the case in lend-lease vessel transfers.

4

Policy Issues

AID HAS BEEN EXTENDED by the United States to some 60 nations, democratic and authoritarian, allied and neutral, developed and underdeveloped, without clear-cut criteria for evaluating competing claims and making the most effective distribution of available resources. Official forecasts of requirements have been lacking and, since the early days of the Marshall Plan, the American people have been in the dark concerning the desirable size and scope of the aid program for even a year or two beyond the 12-month period covered by the latest appropriation request.

Improvised policies and arrangements are tolerable for activities of a temporary, emergency character. Foreign aid, however, has now been a prominent, almost dominant, feature of American foreign relations for more than 15 years and seems likely to continue in being for some years to come. The development of more orderly, better-coordinated policies is therefore essential.

The policy issues selected for exploration in this chapter relate primarily to the use of grants and loans for promoting, in the less developed regions of the world, "better standards of life in larger freedom," [1] because this is gradually becoming the central objective of foreign assistance policy. At the same time, it continues to be an area of controversy insofar as method of financing is concerned. The period of assistance by either loan or grant, for the reconstruction of regions devastated by World War II, is over. The strengthening and subsidizing of military defenses against aggression, to the extent that it remains necessary, is generally conceded to be a field for grant aid.

[1] Charter of the United Nations (preamble).

The chief questions to which this chapter is addressed are: How can country requirements for development aid be estimated? Should development assistance be confined to loans? Is there a need for grant aid? If grants as well as loans are needed, does it matter which activities are financed by which form of aid? How large will country programs be when added together?

How Can Country Requirements for Development Aid be Estimated?

Country requirements for development aid can be estimated by a number of methods, none of which can be described as scientific, objective, or free of political judgments. For the general reader one of the most lucid discussions of the problem is to be found in *Framing a Development Program,* by Gustav F. Papanek. He suggests that the "need for outside assistance depends on the rate of development considered desirable and the extent to which a country can reach that rate using its own resources."[2] After mentioning several ways of establishing a "desirable" rate of development, he, like many others, concludes that no single universal measure exists but that there is much to be said for defining the goal in terms of a desirable rate of increase in per capita income or, as has more recently been suggested, in national income.

The ability of a country to achieve the desired rate of growth is difficult to appraise. Its capacity to mobilize its own resources for development depends on a number of factors, including its per capita income and the ease with which part of this income can be diverted to development, its social structure, administrative competence, political system, values, motivations, and past history. Not only is it difficult to assess the effort that can reasonably be expected from a country, it is even more difficult to determine "how to use outside assistance to increase, not to substitute for, a country's own development effort. . . . If, as a result of outside assistance, a

[2] *Framing a Development Program* (Carnegie Endowment for International Peace, International Conciliation Series No. 527), March 1960, p. 358.

country undertakes to increase its own effort, a major purpose of such help is achieved." [3]

If the desirable rate of development is a 6 per cent per year increase in national income, and if the population of a country is growing at 3 per cent per year, the increase in per capita income would also be about 3 per cent. (If, however, the rate of population increase were reduced to 1.5 per cent, the rise in per capita income could be nearly 4.5 per cent.) If it were estimated that the country could achieve a 4 per cent increase in national income from its own resources, outside technical and financial assistance should, in theory, be equal to one half of any effort the country actually makes itself, up to the absolute amount required to achieve a 6 per cent increase in national income.[4] The target figure could be higher or lower than 6 per cent and could vary from country to country.

The foregoing implies a program rather than a project approach to the promotion of economic growth in the less developed regions. A country, alone or in collaboration with outsiders, establishes its targets or economic goals and frames a medium or long-term program—a 3-, 4-, 5-, or 10-year plan—for reaching those goals. Foreign sources of financial assistance should be equipped to review constructively a proposed country development program or to help prepare a realistic program for an area that does not yet have one. Theoretically, there are then at least two ways of providing such foreign aid as may be required. The first is to provide assistance without attempting to earmark it for particular uses, to offer, for example, a general line of credit, in the expectation that a periodic or continuing review of development progress within the country will indicate whether its resources, domestic as well as foreign, are being used effectively. The second way is to participate in the financing of specific development projects within the over-all program—projects undertaken not because, viewed in isolation, they appear to be "good" projects, but because they fit integrally into the program, because they will move the economy toward its goals, and because they deserve priority within the program.

[3] *Ibid.*, p. 361.
[4] Adapted from *ibid.*, p. 364. No one is more aware than Professor Papanek of the limitations of the procedures he suggests and of the need for modifications and refinements in the course of their application.

The preparation of national development programs may facilitate the calculation of foreign aid requirements, but it raises a fundamental question which troubles many Americans: should the trend toward over-all planning and programming be further encouraged? Because this question is so troublesome, a digression devoted to its consideration may be warranted.

Against Development Programming

Not everyone would agree that the preparation of national development programs is desirable. Examples could be cited of countries that are making excellent progress without development plans and of countries with excellent plans that are making very little progress. Countless unforeseeable circumstances will arise to invalidate the most carefully prepared plans—floods, droughts, war scares, or discoveries of valuable mineral resources in the underdeveloped country; depressions, new inventions, and changes of taste in the industrialized countries with which it trades. Serious miscalculations of a kind that should have been foreseeable will also be made—erroneous estimates of capital requirements for particular undertakings, overestimates of output obtainable from given sectors of the economy, undue optimism or pessimism about price levels. Plans tend to express hopes, and hopes are not evidence of the effectiveness with which resources will in fact be used.

Development programming, its opponents might claim, discourages private enterprise and encourages controls. Planning itself is an unwarranted interference with the laws of supply and demand. The free market is the most efficient allocator of resources. The job of government is to keep it free, not to push or pull the economy in the direction of previously established goals. Governments that set goals will maximize their control over resources in order to reach those goals and, in the process, will become heavily involved in the operation of industry, agriculture, and the services. They may even use their powers to stifle growth that was not anticipated in the original plan but which is no less appropriate than the course of development that was programmed.

Other persons, sharing none of the above views, might still argue against United States encouragement of, or participation in, foreign development planning on the ground that such action creates a presumption that the United States will help underwrite the plans. The plans will postulate investment levels higher than can be met from domestic sources plus private foreign investment. Failure to scale them down to the latter level will constitute an acknowledgement of the need for foreign aid in the amount of the deficit. Even with this amount, we will not know how far along the road to self-sustaining growth and ultimate independence of foreign aid the country will travel. An over-all program—well-balanced and internally consistent though it may be—provides no answer, because no one really knows where the so-called take-off point to self-sustaining growth is located.

Still others would argue that encouragement of development planning will involve us too deeply in the internal affairs of other nations. Virtually every aspect of domestic policy will become a legitimate issue for international discussion; the chances of friction will be greatly increased. Full-scale involvement may be justified in occasional crisis situations, but it should otherwise be avoided.

Although we may not know enough about the process of economic growth to participate with assurance in the preparation and evaluation of over-all development plans, we do know enough to tell whether a proposed fertilizer plant, training institute, or fish hatchery is a good project. By helping to finance good projects that are urgently needed and refusing to finance bad projects, we play a constructive role, while limiting our commitments and retaining greater bargaining freedom. So runs the argument.

For Development Programming

Proponents of a broader approach would point out that foreign financing of good projects may incidentally ease the diversion of domestic resources to bad projects. What matters

> is not whether we finance only "sound" projects in the "right" industries. If the country is financing unsound projects in the wrong industries with its own resources, and is doing so because we have taken care of the sound projects and the right industries, the

net effect of our program is to make possible the unsound projects and the wrong industries.[5]

Moreover, painful choices have to be made among good projects. The reason is two-fold: all the things that need to be done cannot be done at once; yet enough must be done to make a respectable dent in the backlog of problems awaiting solution. The combination of policies and projects adopted should give reasonable promise of providing enough food to feed the hungry, enough job openings to match or exceed the growth in the labor force, enough exports to prevent a balance-of-payments crisis, and so forth. The financing of a power plant here, an agricultural experiment station there, and a cement works at a third point may benefit the surrounding area, but it will be exceedingly difficult to tell whether the bits and pieces add up to "enough" unless they are integrated into an over-all program.

Advocates of development programming necessarily include among them advocates of planning on the Communist model, in which decision-making is highly centralized and failure to fulfill goals can have ghastly consequences for the individuals concerned. This extreme form of planning has its attractions for underdeveloped countries. It would be an egregious error, however, to equate all use of the word "planning" with its most extreme connotations.

Most so-called development programs are far more modest undertakings. They provide a framework within which the country can think in an orderly way about its economic future. Population projections, for example, yield basic data concerning needs for food, clothing, shelter, gainful employment, school facilities, and other essentials. If all school-age children are to be placed in schools, teachers as well as classrooms will be needed. Training teachers is a longer-term, more complex undertaking than building classrooms. School construction takes labor, materials, and capital that might be devoted to residential construction or factory construction. Resources devoted to investment will not be available for consumption. At every point in the exploration, relationships

---

[5] Thomas C. Schelling, "American Aid and Economic Development: Some Critical Issues," in *International Stability and Progress: United States Interests and Instruments* (the American Assembly, Graduate School of Business, Columbia University, 1957), p. 160.

will be revealed which might not otherwise have been so apparent, issues for decision will be clarified, and some of the consequences of alternative decisions will have been anticipated.

Programming does not imply slavish pursuit of a predetermined course but is more analogous to the maneuvering required to keep a heavy airplane aloft and headed for a distant airport: the ability to keep a watchful eye on the controls, to note danger signals, to rechart the course in order to avoid strong headwinds and take advantage of helpful tailwinds, and to maintain at all times the necessary momentum and altitude. Programming of this kind is compatible with wide latitude for private enterprise and is capable of revealing actions that should be taken to liberate and activate the private sector. The free market is in certain cases demonstrably inefficient as an allocator of resources, and in such cases governments have no obligation to remain passive observers of the process.

An annual or semiannual review of progress toward agreed goals can be made. After each review, plans can be adjusted in the light of experience and of more recent information concerning the short- and long-run outlook. The total exercise should give to the country a recurring sense of pace, purpose, and direction, and a series of focal points around which latent energies can be galvanized.

The fact that the nation's plan may have been formulated with United States encouragement need not create a presumption about the availability of United States aid. The International Bank has studied investment possibilities in many countries and produced some of the most distinguished country surveys of the postwar era. It nevertheless finances—and is expected to finance—only a limited range of activities. The more plentiful resources of the United States might give rise to more extravagant hopes in the underdeveloped countries, but this would depend partly on our behavior, including the strength of our commitment to a multilateral, burden-sharing approach.

Many would argue that the most appropriate time for outsiders to influence a country's thinking in constructive ways is precisely when its over-all development program is being formulated or revised, and that it is highly desirable, both from the point of view of the developed and of the underdeveloped countries, to have a projection of aid requirements for several years ahead.

In the United States, the absence of projections increases the unreality of the appropriation process. Year after year, the administration justifies its demand for aid funds by asserting that the sum requested is the absolute minimum required. The amount may be slightly smaller in some respects, and slightly larger in other respects, than the appropriation request of the preceding year. With the proposed appropriation, it is said, stability can be maintained and some further progress made. Without it, disaster will ensue.

The Congress applies its pruning shears vigorously. For a number of years the main effect of the pruning was to reduce the volume of supplies in the pipeline, but the pipeline in due course was reduced to minimum proportions and the possibility of maintaining considerable stability in expenditures in the face of declining appropriations has disappeared.

The public, confused about the goals of the program and the progress, if any, toward those goals, has grown disenchanted with the minuet. Increasingly, it wants to know precisely where we stand. One of the great advantages of the Marshall Plan was that it had an objective (reconstruction), a time limit (four years), and a price tag ($17 billion). With respect to economic development, however, we do not seem to know for sure where we are going, when we hope to get there, how much the trip will cost, or who will pay for the tickets.

Even when the objective was restoration of prewar levels of production in a fairly homogeneous area, Western Europe, the requirements for foreign aid, as initially estimated in 1947 by the Committee for European Economic Cooperation, turned out to be fairly wide of the mark. Their value was more political than economic. They "proved" that the job was within the capabilities of the countries concerned and they provided a rough standard for measuring progress.

Similar projections of requirements for development assistance would be more difficult to make, but not impossible. A national development program that includes effective measures for raising export earnings to the level needed to finance imports by some designated future year, suggests a possible terminal date for foreign aid to that country. Greater assurance of the availability of aid during the interim would itself introduce an element of stability into development programming that has to date been sadly lacking.

The Program Approach

It was suggested earlier that the major objective of development programs might be defined in terms of a rate of growth in the national income. Why not a rate that would permit a 6 per cent per year rise in per capita income instead of the more frequently mentioned 2 per cent? Cannot shortages of trained personnel, an oft-cited limitation on the capacity of underdeveloped countries to absorb capital, be overcome by importing them from abroad? More technical assistance may enable countries to utilize more capital assistance, and the increased capital assistance may raise the demand for technical assistance.

The economies of the less developed countries are neither as flexible nor as inflexible as some may suppose. Shortages of technicians and inadequacies of public administration do tend to set ceilings on the amount of capital that can be used effectively. Such shortages and inadequacies cannot readily be overcome by importing personnel.

Skilled and professional personnel cannot be obtained in self-sustaining units like military divisions and at the same time be integrated into the economic life of the receiving country. Development is not just a matter of getting roads built, ports improved, and fertilizer spread, but of changing values, habits, and institutions so that the people themselves will be capable of the full range of actions necessary for continuously improving their levels of living. The role of the foreigner under this generally accepted interpretation of development is educational—and temporary. He offers guidance with respect to policies, he demonstrates and advises, he assists in the creation of new institutions.

Foreigners can help to prepare both over-all development plans and individual project proposals that appear to be well conceived, technically feasible, and of recognizable importance to the economic and social advancement of the area. To carry them out, they need heirs in the form of "opposite numbers"; they cannot serve merely as alien employers of local labor.

The desire that supervisory and executive positions be held by nationals of the developing country is part and parcel of the revolution of rising expectations. Any government that frustrated this desire by allowing foreigners to hold more than, say, 10 per cent of the key posts would probably be in political trouble on the home front even though the result might be to increase significantly the amount of new capital that could be invested productively. Countries consequently should not normally be allowed to inflate their need for grants and loans by planning to import large numbers of foreigners for operational rather than for educational functions. They should be encouraged, however, to prepare along with their capital investment programs, parallel manpower programs for training the requisite number of semiskilled, skilled, and professional personnel of various kinds.

In almost every underdeveloped country capital is scarce, but in most of them unskilled labor is plentiful. In such instances, it will be to the country's advantage to increase its wealth by maximum utilization of the available labor supply—through voluntary labor service, youth corps, community development programs, assignment of armed forces personnel to conservation and road-building projects, and other devices. Foreign assistance, technical and financial, should be employed to stimulate domestic efforts to use productively the most abundant resource of the underdeveloped countries—their reservoir of unskilled labor.

Previous rates of capital investment set practical limits on future rates. Rarely would an underdeveloped country be capable of doubling in a three-year period the volume of productive investment attained in the best three of the preceding ten years. Exceptions would tend to be countries so small and primitive that a single development project would loom very large in the national statistics. At the other end of the scale, exceptions might occur among countries already well on the road to self-sustaining growth. Thus another criterion for reviewing and setting ceilings on requests for foreign aid might be the rate of investment attained by the country in some recent good years plus a margin for improvement.

Developed countries habitually tend to devote approximately 15 per cent of their national income to capital formation; underdeveloped countries characteristically devote less than 10 per cent. Part of the problem is to step up the rates of capital formation in underdeveloped countries in an effort to attain what W. W. Rostow has called the "take-off" into self-sustaining growth. It does not follow from this that the role of foreign aid is simply to inject, for investment, predetermined amounts of capital into an economy. The quality of investment is every bit as important as the quantity. The breaking of some bottleneck within an underdeveloped country—say, a set of attitudes—may be the key to increasing its rate of capital formation. In such cases, foreign aid will be better employed as a catalyst in attacking the attitudes that discourage agricultural or industrial investment than in direct investment.

The investment requirements of underdeveloped countries are frequently calculated on the assumption that each additional $3.00 or $3.50 devoted to productive investment will add $1.00 to annual output. If the capital/output ratio is assumed to be 3:1, then enabling a country to invest 12 per cent of its national product in fixed capital would permit total output to grow at the rate of 4 per cent per year—or 2 per cent per capita if population were growing concurrently at 2 per cent per year. A 15 per cent rate of investment would permit a 5 per cent per year increase in national product. Depending on whether population were growing at the rate of 3, 2, or 1.5 per cent per year, per capita income would double in 35, 24, or 20 years—still assuming the 15 per cent rate of investment and 5 per cent growth in national product.

The assumption that the capital/output ratio must be about the same for countries at comparable stages of development and that the ratio will remain constant for an extended period of time is an unsafe one. There is no satisfactory substitute for an inductive, on-the-spot build-up of investment requirements, country by country, along with records of the productivity of the investments actually made.

The preparation of a development program, it is obvious, is a complex and laborious undertaking. Moreover, it involves judgments on many matters that far transcend the realm of economics. Economic criteria do not exist for assessing the efforts being made to obtain optimum use of local manpower, to evaluate the requirements of defense as against development, or consumption versus investment, or the dangers of inflation versus a slower rate of growth. The "political" answer will vary from country to country, and the decisions reached may not prove equally satisfying to the underdeveloped country and to the outside sources from which the underdeveloped country hopes to obtain aid. The basic requirement is that the development program deserve and receive widespread support from within the country. Unless it meets in substantial measure the felt needs of the people of the area, its contribution to political stability and probably to economic growth as well will be reduced, regardless of the approval it commands from abroad.

From the point of view of the rest of the world, there are additional requirements, but they can best be stated negatively: that the program is not too unrealistic, economically speaking, and that realization will not jeopardize international peace and security. That it conform more positively with United States or United Nations concepts of sound economic and political policy is not essential *ab initio*. If a basis for collaboration is established, time and experience may bridge the remaining gap in viewpoint.

The Project Approach

If the country really has an investment program ready for execution, the program will consist in large part of concrete projects for each of which equipment, manpower, and capital are needed. Conventions whereby foreign aid is tied to certain of these projects provide focal points for discussions in depth and avoid unnecessary political embarrassments. It is easier to supply tractors under an aid program and to let the receiving country use its own resources to bring in passenger automobiles than to appear to be equally responsible for both imports. It is more satisfying to make possible a particular harbor improvement than to contribute the same sum to an over-all development program that includes improving the harbor in question. Moreover, the likelihood is greater that the harbor will be properly improved if attention is focussed directly on that undertaking than if harbor improvement is on a par with virtually everything else in the development program. Not everything in the program will be equally well done, and the demonstration effects of a few well-executed projects may be very great.

The project approach helps to establish ground rules acceptable to both parties. It provides a mechanism for linking technical assistance with capital assistance. After some informal discussion, one party requests commodities, or equipment, or experts for a stated purpose; the other makes them available for that purpose and thereby identifies itself with a particular undertaking. The difference between success and failure of the undertaking is more likely to rest in what are regarded by the inexperienced as bothersome details than in the broad design. Foreign aid can be made conditional upon the completion of prior engineering surveys or market surveys, the employment of qualified management, the allocation of domestic resources in specified amounts, and other actions that help to guarantee competent supervision and execution of the project. The odds will be improved that at least the project in question will receive the supplies and the attention that it needs. Successful projects provide, at local levels, visible evidence of international collaboration.

Historically, the project approach has not meant financing a fixed proportion of the total cost of designated projects *within* a development program, but rather financing the *foreign exchange* costs of specific undertakings that seem well enough conceived to merit outside aid. The underdeveloped country has been given an incentive for the prosecution of projects having a relatively high foreign exchange content: for manufacturing establishments in preference to schools, for railways instead of roads, for processes that are capital-intensive rather than labor-intensive. Foreign aid has become the sum of the foreign exchange requirements of these projects, a sum unlikely to equal the resources deficit of the economy as a whole.

The project approach satisfies demands for action and enables some inherently desirable undertakings to be initiated without waiting for agreement on a total program. For economic growth to take place, growing points must be established. Growth will be an erratic process at best and the interdependence of different developmental activities can be exaggerated.

Nevertheless, the absence of a larger framework within which to judge the need for help on a particular project or group of projects is serious. Without it, meaningful priorities cannot be established and the composition of technical assistance and development efforts is likely to be determined more by the bureaucratic strength of the agencies involved than by the need to make the most efficient use of resources.[6] Moreover, the adequacy of the proposed level of foreign aid for the country as a whole will be harder to judge without the projections of gainful employment, capital formation, national income, and other basic ingredients of a development plan.

Fortunately, the project approach and the program approach are not mutually exclusive. Some resources may be provided in the form of grants or credits for specific projects and the balance as nonproject aid. If the over-all development program of the country is to be fulfilled, the total amount of foreign aid provided under either approach, or under any combination of the two approaches, should equal the difference between import requirements and export potentials. Or, to state the same thing another way, total aid should equal the difference between the anticipated total cost of the investments to be made and the expected level of domestic savings plus private foreign investment.

In a sense, the best of both worlds—fulfillment of the country program while creating a series of lasting monuments to international economic collaboration—will be achieved if aid is made available for "good projects" in amounts that add up to the resources deficit of the country for the period covered by the program. This happy outcome will not always be attainable because some countries need budget support, food imports, and other assistance which cannot readily be identified with specific projects.

Should Development Assistance Be Confined to Loans?

Should lending be the only form of public aid available to cover the resources deficit? In other words, should the resources deficit of a country program be held down to the amount that the country

[6] Papanek, *op. cit.*, p. 334. See also the balance of his discussion of "Separate Appraisal of Projects and Fields," pp. 331-35.

can reasonably expect to service as foreign debt and should the "desirable rate of development" for that country be determined accordingly?

At the project level, it makes little difference whether the extra financing that enables the government to include the project in its development program takes the form of a hard loan, a soft loan, or a grant. The end-user usually pays in local currency for what he gets. Neither his morality nor the efficiency of his enterprise is directly affected by the form of aid his government has negotiated.[7]

The United States Government, especially its legislative branch, has nevertheless wanted government-supplied capital for foreign economic development to take the form of loans. As far back as 1954, the President's message on the mutual security bill recommended gradually replacing grant aid with loan aid. A respected Senator, urging a speed-up in the process, said during the debate that he thought "it would be better to lend them the money and never get it back than simply give it away to them, because we, at least, put the transaction on a businesslike basis when we lend them the money; and when we give it away, make a gift of it, it is not on such a basis."[8]

More recently, the administration has been placed under congressional mandate to bring about an end to grant aid for economic development. The reasons include not only the belief that lending is more "businesslike" and that loans are more likely to evoke "sound" economic and financial policies in the borrowing country than other forms of aid, but that grant aid may corrupt receiving governments even though the ultimate recipients within their territories pay in full for the goods they get.

There is probably also a widespread feeling that limiting aid to loans that have to be repaid will set a ceiling on the amount of aid requested but will not unduly inhibit economic growth. Just as an individual should limit his acquisitions to items that he can pay

[7] See Chapter 1. An exception is the private enterprise such as the Tata Iron and Steel Company that borrows abroad and must buy with rupees the dollars or other foreign currency needed to repay its debt. In the event of a depreciation in the Indian currency, the company would have to put up more rupees to meet its obligations. This would also be true if it had negotiated a loan repayable in local currency but containing a maintenance-of-value clause.

[8] *Congressional Record,* Vol. 100, Pt. 9 (1954), p. 12513.

for outright or buy on credit, so a nation must relate its ambitions to its resources and earning capacity. If credit is obtained and put to productive use, output will rise and incomes will increase. If the loan was worth making or taking, the increase should be more than sufficient to provide for payment of interest and amortization of principal.[9]

The rise in domestic output, however, may not generate the necessary amount of foreign exchange. Furthermore, resources that have to be devoted to external payments will not be available for consumption or investment at home. The transfer will slow down the potential rate of development below what it would be if the aid were as efficiently used with no obligation concerning repayment.

The central questions about development via the loan route are, therefore, whether growth will be rapid enough and whether it will be the right kind. A heavy concentration of investment in export industries may simplify loan repayment, but heavy concentration in education may establish a more promising foundation for long-run economic growth and political democracy. The United States doctrine that development loans are preferable to grants in virtually all circumstances does not seem to be the result of searching analysis of the rate of progress most likely to promote the general welfare, or of careful study of the debt-servicing capacity of the underdeveloped countries.

> Obviously if foreign assistance must be repaid, the debtor country will have a correspondingly smaller amount of resources available for further capital formation. It would seem to follow from this that the main factor in the decision as to whether a country should get a loan or a grant depends upon the magnitude of its need for capital. . . . The basic questions are . . . how important it is to have the country use for further capital formation the additional resources that would be at its disposal if repayment is not required, and how likely it is that these resources will actually be used for that purpose. In some cases, resources that would be needed to repay loans would be a substantial por-

---

[9] "The committee believes that if the development of other countries derives from a judicious use of their own resources and sound fiscal policies, capital provided from this country [the United States] to assist in the process can and should ultimately be repaid. . . . gifts generate dependence whereas loans encourage independence." *Foreign Aid*, Report of Special Senate Committee to Study the Foreign Aid Program, S. Rept. 300, 85 Cong. 1 sess. (1957), p. 15.

tion of an underdeveloped country's net capital formation, and the need to repay might significantly slow up the development process.[10]

That present rates of development are not rapid enough is often asserted, but there is little knowledge of what would be rapid enough. A number of experts assume or imply that a 2 per cent per annum increase in real per capita income, the approximate rate attained by the United States between 1870 and 1929, would be tolerable. It would mean a 50 per cent increase in 20 years, a 100 per cent increase, or a doubling of present standards, in 35 years.

> The statistical income per person in the 100 [underdeveloped] countries and territories in the year 1950 averaged approximately $90. It probably reached slightly over $100 per person in 1959. Gross income grew at the rate of 3 per cent a year, but because there were 200,000,000 more mouths to feed in these countries in 1959 than there were in 1950, the net increase in income per person was only about 1 per cent, that is, about $1 a year. This is too slow—dangerously so.
>
> We are now starting the crucial decade of the 1960's. Clearly economic growth in the less developed countries should be speeded. The first task of each nation is to set its own goal and carry out its own program for achieving it. But, in addition, I propose that the nations of the world set for themselves the common task of assisting the people of the underdeveloped areas to increase the annual growth of their per capita income from one to two per cent each year for the next ten years. This means roughly an increase of $2 per head per year, instead of the present rate of $1 per head. . . . This is a modest, but a reasonable and feasible goal.[11]

But is 2 per cent "enough"? In 1995 when average per capita income in the underdeveloped countries at 1959 prices reaches $200, per capita income in the United States, if it also increases at 2 per cent per year, will have reached $5400. The gap, in absolute terms, will have widened enormously, and international stability may be

[10] Walter S. Salant, "Some Basic Considerations of Public Finance in the Economic Development of Underdeveloped Countries," a paper presented to the annual meeting of the International Institute of Public Finance, London, September 1951, pp. 11-12 (processed). Mr. Salant calls attention in a footnote to the *Report to the President on Foreign Economic Policies* (Gray Report), Nov. 10, 1950, p. 67, where a similar point of view is expressed.

[11] Paul G. Hoffman, *One Hundred Countries, One and One Quarter Billion People* (Albert D. and Mary Lasker Foundation, 1960), p. 10.

in greater jeopardy than it is today. Would 3 per cent be enough? Can the underdeveloped nations earn the foreign exchange to pay service charges on loans and still invest enough to permit development at a politically tolerable rate? Can they grow to the point where net repayment will not be demanded? Will they become such good risks that new loans can be obtained to pay off old ones and a floating debt of sizable proportions can be maintained?

Forecasting Requirements

The amount of foreign debt that can be serviced by an economy undergoing profound structural change can be forecast only within a wide range. The lower end of the range—identified on the following chart as AX—would represent the consensus of conservative estimates of the country's growth and export earnings. The upper end of the range, which might be 25 to 30 per cent higher, and includes the XY area of the chart, would represent a consensus based on more optimistic assumptions.

So long as foreign indebtedness remains in the AX range, the chances of repayment are good. This is therefore the area for what might be thought of as the holders of first mortgages, i.e., private bondholders and public lending institutions such as the World Bank and the Export-Import Bank. The area between X and Y is, so to speak, for the second mortgage holders, the institutions willing to take some risks beyond those permitted the conventional lending agencies. To anticipate our discussion, there might be a still higher point on the scale, "Z," representing either the country's absorptive capacity for capital or its estimated requirements in order to increase national income by an agreed percentage per year. Z minus Y would then represent the need for grant aid.

In this review, the point has been made that economic development is a product of the effectiveness with which the total resources of a country are used, not just of the effectiveness with which foreign aid funds are used. Similarly, the ability of a developing country to service foreign loans does not depend upon which industries or which projects are financed by the loans but on whether all industries and services together earn enough foreign exchange to pay for essential imports and provide a surplus that can be applied to debt-servicing.

CHART 1. *Estimated Requirements of Country N for Foreign Aid, 1960-65*

Hard Loans	Soft Loans	Grants

A   X   Y   Z

LEGEND

AZ = estimated requirements of Country N for foreign aid during the period 1960-65, on the basis of an agreed program to increase the national income by, say, 6 per cent per year during 1961-66. AZ does not represent the total cost of the investments to be made but the amount after subtracting the resources to be provided domestically and the resources to be provided by foreign private investment and private remittances. Failure on the part of Country N to mobilize domestic resources to the extent believed feasible should result in a corresponding reduction in the amount of foreign aid made available.

AX = portion of the aid requirements of Country N which should be obtained in the form of conventional loans from public lending agencies (15- to 25-year terms, 4 to 6 per cent interest). AX, in other words, represents the additional foreign exchange debt that can be serviced, in the light of obligations already incurred and conservative, long-term projections of the export earnings of Country N.

AY = portion of the aid requirements that could be met by borrowing from abroad if somewhat more optimistic assumptions concerning the credit-worthiness and probable export earnings of Country N could reasonably be made. XY is therefore an area for loans on easier terms than those of the conventional lending agencies.

YZ = AZ minus AY = the balance needed if the agreed rate of growth is to be achieved without imposing an excessively heavy burden of debt on Country N. YZ, a residual subject to even wider margins of error than the other components of aid requirements, indicates the portion of total requirements to be met by grant aid.

Loans Repayable in the Currency of the Lender

It is clear, on the one hand, that the possibilities of further international lending of the kind engaged in by the International Bank are by no means exhausted. It is equally clear, on the other hand, that certain countries are already fairly heavily saddled with external debt and may be approaching the limits of their borrowing power.[12] Unlike dividend payments, service payments on conventional public loans have to be met irrespective of fluctuations in export earnings. In several Latin American countries, service payments on public debt alone have recently been taking more than 10 per cent of earnings from abroad. In India, more than $1 billion will be required for the repayment of external debt (total external debt, not public debt alone) during the period covered by India's Third Five Year Plan. Because of this obligation, foreign aid requirements will be nearly 25 per cent greater than the $4.4 billion believed necessary for the import of capital goods during 1961-65.[13]

The wisdom of burdening some of the newly independent African nations with external debt at this stage of their struggle for survival is also questionable. If loans are made first, and then grants (or new public loans) have to be made later to enable the country to meet its obligations with respect to outstanding loans, the grants (or new loans) may well be larger, because of the necessity of covering interest as well as principal, than if the principal sums had been offered as grants in the first place.

The burden on export earnings of loans repayable in the currency of the lender is, of course, a function of the terms of the loans as well as their volume—their total length, the length of the period of grace before principal repayments are demanded, and the rate of interest. A 40-year loan repayable in equal annual installments, with interest at 2½ per cent on the outstanding balance, means annual payments substantially smaller than those on a similar 20-year loan at 5 per cent interest. A 50-year, interest-free loan requires far smaller annual payments than a 40-year, 2½ per cent loan.

[12] See Chapter 2.
[13] Based on figures contained in *India, Economic Newsletter*, April 1960 (Embassy of India, Washington).

At present, to maintain the solvency of the public agencies making hard loans, rates of interest on such loans tend to reflect the cost of raising capital in the capital-exporting nation, plus certain special charges added by the lending agency. So long as the United States Government has authority to make grants as well as loans, the effective rate of interest on development capital can be substantially lowered by combining grant aid with loan aid. If the policy now is to eliminate grant aid for economic development, while the Soviet Union continues to provide loan aid at 2 or 2½ per cent interest, a revision of interest rates may be in order.

The length of public loans today is frequently determined by the life-expectancy of the equipment being furnished. The theory is that the generator or locomotive should pay for itself during its lifetime. If the loan were viewed, however, not as the basis for the purchase of generators or locomotives, but as an equivalent contribution to the development program of the low-income country, made in an effort to maximize the rate of development obtainable before recourse to grant aid, the case for longer-term loans would be much stronger.

As noted in the discussion of the project approach to development financing—

> Where the problem is one of inadequacy of resources, it cannot be met simply by providing foreign loans or grants to pay for imported equipment. And there is the danger that countries will distort their investment programs to qualify for foreign aid available for imported equipment. Instead of giving priority to the most important projects, which may have a very small content of imported equipment, there will be a tendency to give priority to spectacular projects for which foreign aid is available because it has a larger content of imported equipment. Or, if the more important projects are given priority, they will be undertaken in a manner that uses imported equipment wastefully where local labor and materials could be used more economically.[14]

To summarize some already oversimplified statements concerning development financing via hard loans:

---

[14] *Economic Development with Stability*, a Report to the Government of India by a Mission of the International Monetary Fund (1953), p. 71.

In the light of the agreed social and economic objectives of Country N, estimates can be made of the required rates of capital formation and of the amount of foreign exchange that the country can reasonably be expected to devote to the servicing of foreign debt during a given future period of years. The actual amount of debt that can be serviced will depend, among other things, on the terms of the loans—the easier the terms, the greater the burden that can be carried. Appropriate assumptions concerning the probable terms of such loans can be made on the basis of existing knowledge of the limitations of the conventional lending agencies. The volume of hard loans that a country can safely assume responsibility for servicing would thus be ascertained.

If no other external financing were obtainable, countries with more ambitious programs would either have to squeeze more out of their domestic economies or cut back their development programs. As of the present, India and Pakistan would probably have to lower their sights dangerously. The newly independent African nations, whose credit is not yet established and whose domestic resources are in some cases extremely limited, would be in a bad way. Those Latin American countries that are already devoting a sizable fraction of their foreign exchange earnings to the servicing of external debt would be unable to borrow more unless their export prospects brightened perceptibly. Countries with the most glowing export prospects would tend to get the most development assistance.

Conventional lending agencies expect to be repaid in full. They accumulate reserves against contingencies but, in order for these institutions to remain in business, the overwhelming majority of their loans must be repaid approximately as scheduled. Occasionally, a rescheduling of the debt may be feasible. Failure to service outstanding hard loans will be a serious matter because it will almost inevitably shut down completely, or reduce to a trickle, the inflow of foreign private capital and disqualify the country from access to conventional sources of public loan aid during the period of default.

Loans Repayable in the Currency of the Borrower

The XY area on the chart (page 96) represents debt that a developing country may be able to service if somewhat more optimistic assumptions are made concerning its economic prospects. In our suggested procedure for estimating foreign aid requirements, it becomes the area for the Development Loan Fund, for P.L. 480 loans, for the International Development Association, and for the lending agencies prepared to take greater risks than the International Bank. In this range, inability to repay debts should not classify the borrowing country as a defaulter on its international obligations, provided it is making a reasonable developmental effort and takes seriously not only the servicing of senior securities but also the portion of the junior securities that it is judged able to service.

The designation of junior securities as those repayable in the currency of the borrower is politically convenient though not economically necessary. Differences in expectations concerning true repayment could be reflected in other ways and, in the lending of the International Development Association, it is expected that they will be.

The current procedures for determining the volume of lending on terms more flexible than those of the conventional lending agencies bear little resemblance to the suggested procedures. The volume of soft loans is now established primarily by the vigor and success of American efforts to dispose of surplus agricultural commodities. The object of American negotiators is to arrange for constructive use abroad of surpluses that might otherwise be running up storage bills at home, while avoiding the charge that outright gifts are being made. The United States accepts local currencies in payment. It reserves 10 to 35 per cent of these for United States uses, whether or not the amount thus set aside is really needed by United States agencies and enterprises. It then lends back as much of the remainder, the country-use portion, as the purchasing nation can be persuaded to borrow. P.L. 480 loans are the product of these negotiations.

Concurrently, the Development Loan Fund makes its loans for specific projects, after satisfying itself that the projects will enlarge national income sufficiently to permit repayment in local currency. (DLF loans are dollar credits but, in more than 75 per cent of the loans and guaranties approved, are repayable in the currency of the borrower.) The probability that the country will ultimately be able to sacrifice enough foreign exchange to repay in real resources its outstanding P.L. 480, DLF, and other local currency loans is rarely assessed with care. Future negotiations, it is hoped, will result in mutually acceptable arrangements for true repayment— or for new local currency loans or a total or partial write-off of the debt.

Failure to relate local currency lending more definitely to repayment prospects and persistent illusions regarding the character-building qualities of loans that are not loans lie at the root of many present difficulties. The peculiar features of the open-ended system in vogue today are: for the borrowing country, the comparative ease of making payments in its own currency; for the lending country, the accumulation of a growing volume of the borrower's inconvertible currency; and for both borrower and lender, the indefiniteness of the arrangements for translating the accumulation into a more meaningful form of repayment.

The advantage to the borrowing country of making payment in its own currency is that while so doing it will not suffer a corresponding loss in real resources. In the case of a 40-year loan, this means an extended breathing spell. The disadvantage is political— the potential embarrassment over having a foreign government gain possession of substantial amounts of its currency and thereby become able to frustrate its monetary and development policies in unforeseen ways. In a political world, embarrassment on the part of a borrowing government, whether justified or unjustified, may prove embarrassing also to the lending government.

Warnings of future difficulties from growing American accumulations of foreign currencies have been sounded in numerous American reports on the foreign aid program. Loans "repayable in the inconvertible currencies of foreign nations are undesirable, and the practice of granting them should be terminated. Our relations with other countries will suffer from United States control of large amounts of their currencies."[15] The United States "has not yet developed adequate policies to deal with the accumulation and use

---

[15] *Report to the President by the President's Citizen Advisers on the Mutual Security Program* (Fairless Committee), Mar. 1, 1957, p. 10.

of local currency holdings resulting from sales of surplus agricultural commodities and from loan repayments." [16]

Projections have been made to indicate that, under present policies, with relending of principal and interest received in repayment of earlier loans, United States accumulations of foreign currencies will reach astronomical totals by the end of the century—between $37 billion and $154 billion.[17] The miracle of compound interest, applied in this fashion, without comparable projections of national incomes, money in circulation, etc., and without greater allowance for the erratic nature of public policy, inevitably exaggerates the problem.

Conservative estimates of local currency indebtedness to the United States in 1963 (cash balances plus outstanding loans) place the total at $9 to $10 billion. As of June 30, 1959, over 60 per cent of the total accumulation of the United States was in the currencies of seven countries: Greece, India, Indonesia, Israel, Pakistan, Spain, and Yugoslavia. In a number of areas, the portion set aside for United States use—the 10 per cent reserved for government agencies to purchase from the Treasury—was already large enough in 1959 to cover the anticipated needs of the United States Government for many years ahead: 15 years in the case of Israel, 18 in India, and 37 in Yugoslavia. In the opinion of the Department of the Treasury, an accumulation sufficient to cover needs for two full years ahead is adequate.[18]

Some of the United States holding will have to be written off. Depending upon the political and economic situation of the United States at the time, Americans may feel disillusioned and deceived. If the write-off takes the form of granting some of the United States-owned local currency to the developing country, it will have to be

[16] *Third Interim Report of President's Committee to Study the United States Military Assistance Program* (Draper Committee), July 13, 1959, p. 27.

[17] Robert L. Berenson, William M. Bristol, and Ralph I. Strauss, *Accumulation and Administration of Local Currencies,* a Special Report to James H. Smith, Jr., Director, International Cooperation Administration, August 1958, p. iv.

[18] *The Problem of Excess Accumulation of U.S.-Owned Local Currencies,* Findings and Recommendations Submitted to the Under Secretary of State by the Consultants on International Finance and Economic Problems, Apr. 4, 1960 (Mason Report), p. 4, and App. I, p. 5.

borne in mind that the commodities that gave rise to the accumulation will long ago have been consumed, and the receiving country will not be enriched in any real sense by acquiring title to an additional quantity of the currency that it could print if it wished to.

The grant will not finance increased imports. It therefore cannot serve as a substitute for dollar aid. This point was made forcefully by the local currency consultants in their special report to the ICA Director in the summer of 1958:

> During the past two years the Congress has cut dollar appropriations for foreign assistance on the stated grounds that they were not needed where large accumulations of local currencies are available. This reflects a lack of understanding of the fact that these local currencies cannot substitute for U.S. aid dollars.[19]

According to later congressional hearings on the mutual security appropriation, the lack of understanding was still widespread in 1960. It is insufficiently appreciated that an additional supply of its own inconvertible currency is of no help to a developing country in obtaining needed imports.

> In spite of the fact that these local currencies do not constitute a physical resource to the host country . . . it does not follow that they are valueless to the U.S. The U.S., in cooperation with the host country, can use these currencies to help accelerate development. This may be done by investing such currencies in long-range activities that otherwise might be difficult or impossible for the host country to carry out, for political or other reasons.[20]

In other words, it is not always easy for the host country to mobilize its own currency and put it to optimum use. The sale of the surplus by the United States provides us with an opportunity to discuss how and where the commodities themselves will be used. The loan of the local currency proceeds affords further chances for joint discussion and programming. The ultimate disposition of the payments received in amortization of the loan provides still another chance.

These built-in requirements for joint planning are considered by

---

[19] Berenson, Bristol, and Strauss, *op. cit.*, p. 9.
[20] *Ibid.*, pp. 10-11.

some knowledgeable and sophisticated people to be adequate justification for making sales payable in inconvertible currencies, even if such sales turn out overwhelmingly to have been grants rather than loans. The implication that granting the commodities would deprive us of opportunities for joint programming, however, assumes a greater difference between grants and loans than there really is. If commodity grants were made, counterpart deposits could, and in all probability would, be required. The host country, not the United States, would own the counterpart, but the drawing down of the account would still require approval or absence of objection from the United States.

That joint programming is desirable is often taken for granted. Where differences of opinion arise, however, the compromises reached may on occasion be worse than the independent decisions of the developing country would have been. Even wrong decisions, for which the government of the developing country has to assume full responsibility, may be preferable at times to right decisions taken under the tutelage of a major power. Most of the time, however, the broad experience of the United States or of an international agency can usefully be brought to bear on the economic problems of a developing country, particularly at the moment that the surplus commodities or other real resources are imported.

The intensity of the collaboration will depend on the general political outlook of the developing country, on its need for technical and financial assistance from abroad, on the spirit in which the assistance is offered, and on the total amount received. It will not in reality depend to any important extent on the portion of the foreign assistance that takes the form of loans repayable in local currency. The volume of such loans consequently should not be determined by assumed advantages in the field of programming, nor by the size of our agricultural surpluses, nor by self-imposed restrictions against graciously granting today what we will grudgingly grant tomorrow.

Instead, progressively more scientific efforts should be made to estimate the borrowing nation's debt-servicing capacity on two assumptions concerning its economic and political prospects: conservative assumptions (to point X on the requirements chart, page 96), and more optimistic assumptions (to point Y). Hard loans plus soft loans should not exceed the amount of external debt the country can carry on the basis of the more optimistic assumptions. If the soft loans take the form of credits repayable in local currency, the ceiling figure for such loans (AY minus AX) would be known, and the fears of vast accumulations of domestic currency in the hands of foreigners might subside. If the borrowing country makes good economic progress, it may agree to permit conversion of the lender's local currency accounts at the official rate of exchange. Except for the length of the period of grace preceding conversion, the loan will then have been a loan in the normal sense of the term, repaid in goods and services.

If the more optimistic assumptions prove unjustified, the local currency loans will have to be scaled down or extended. Inability to release the full equivalent in foreign exchange, however, should not categorize the debtor nation as in default of its international obligations, provided it has made a reasonable effort to mobilize and utilize the resources at its disposal. It should continue, for example, to be eligible for loans from the World Bank.

Is There Need for Grant Aid?

Analyses of investment requirements and of debt-servicing capacities would probably show that tolerable rates of economic progress in some free-world countries could not be made on the basis of mobilizable domestic resources, private foreign investment, and public loans from abroad, including soft loans up to the limits for which there were reasonable prospects of ultimate repayment in real terms. These countries would be candidates for grant aid. Their total requirements would exceed point Y on the chart and extend to some higher point, Z.

Estimates of requirements for grant aid (AZ minus AY) will be subject to a wider margin of error than any other estimates in development programming. This is because most of the other projections can be built up inductively from agreed (or accepted) starting points concerning population growth, savings rates, tax yields, export earnings, defense and housing programs, and so forth.

Requirements for foreign financing, however, are customarily derived as a residual—they are the gap between investment needs and investment resources. The gap can be filled by equity or portfolio investment from private foreign sources, by hard loans from public agencies, by soft loans from such agencies, or by grant aid. The need for grant aid is the residual after all the other imponderables have been weighed. Nevertheless, on the understanding that countries able to attain and maintain adequate levels of capital formation without grant aid would not receive grant aid, and that the purpose of grant aid, when given, was to ease the burden of nations committed to a substantial independent effort (not to reward those making unsubstantial efforts), crude limits to requirements for grant aid could be calculated, country by country.

India is perhaps the leading candidate for grant aid. A detailed analysis of its economic situation and prospects in a recent issue of *The Economist* confirms the need for substantially more foreign assistance during the course of the Third Five Year Plan than India can afford in the form of credits:

> One last need is that the aid programme should not unduly add to India's foreign indebtedness. In the second plan nearly half of the assistance has taken the form of "hard" loans and credits, repayable in foreign currencies. It is an open question how much more "hard" debt India could undertake without incurring some loss of confidence in its financial soundness. At present, it does not look as though more than half the possible aid for the third plan will be in the form of grants or of "soft" loans repayable in rupees.[21]

Pakistan, Vietnam, Burma, and the newly independent countries of Africa are also candidates for grant aid. Furthermore, as reported earlier, there are several Latin American countries that are already devoting a fairly high proportion of their foreign exchange earnings to debt repayment.

American policy from 1954 through 1960 was gradually to close the door to grant aid for economic development from mutual security appropriations. While the front door was being locked, a trap door remained—and remains—open through the Agricultural

---

[21] *The Economist*, Mar. 26, 1960, p. 1285.

Trade Development and Assistance Act (P.L. 480). Title I, Section 104(e), of that act permits grants for economic development to be made from the local currency proceeds of sales of surplus agricultural commodities. Commitments under such grants amounted to the equivalent of almost a quarter of a billion dollars as of June 30, 1959 [22] and more than half a billion dollars one year later. Because giving away the local currencies is such an obvious way of preventing embarrassing accumulations in the hands of the United States, it is reasonable to assume that this particular authority to make grants will be used increasingly in the future.

It should be recognized, however, that if we give back to the buyer the currency with which he bought the commodities in the first place, we have given him the commodities. The hocus-pocus of selling the commodities for local currency and granting only the currency should not mislead us.

The pros and cons of making grants of surplus commodities, *ab initio*, for development purposes deserve more serious consideration. From the beginning, Title II of P.L. 480 has authorized grants of surplus commodities to help friendly nations meet famine or other urgent or extraordinary relief requirements. This title was amended in mid-1960 to permit grants for economic development during the ensuing fiscal year, but the expenditure ceiling was left unchanged and objections were expressed in the Congress to the use of Title II for anything except famine and disaster relief.[23] The mutual security legislation likewise permits grant aid in special and emergency situations while discouraging its use for economic development.

If the front door to grant aid for economic development is plainly open, the receiving government may remain uneasy about accepting grants, despite statistical and economic "proof" of its requirements

---

[22] International Cooperation Administration, *U.S. External Assistance, Obligations and Other Commitments, July 1, 1945, through June 30, 1959* (1960), p. 1, and *Operations Report*, June 30, 1960, p. 101. According to the latter source, sales agreements signed under Title I of P.L. 480 as of June 30, 1960, amounted to $4.8 billion, of which $2.2 billion was committed to loans to foreign governments under Sec. 104(g), $327 million to Cooley amendment loans to private enterprise, $528 million to grants under Sec. 104(e), and the remainder reserved for various other uses.

[23] *Congressional Record*, daily ed., May 2, 1960, pp. 8383, 8386-7.

for such aid. Its people may have difficulty believing that the only *quid pro quo* is orderly pursuit of the agreed development program. They may feel that, because something of value has been obtained, something extra is expected of them. The donor nation may have reinforced their feeling by implying that, as donor, it ought to realize special benefits of some kind. The result may be strain and irritation on both sides.

The strain may be accepted as a cost of bilateral programs of development assistance, to be weighed against the benefits. Except for the length of time during which it may be needed, there is little inherent difference between grant aid for development and grant aid for famine relief, for reconstruction, and for other purposes for which it has been, and continues to be, extended. "Grant aid has been a widely used instrument of foreign policy throughout history, has served United States interests over the postwar years, and should not be foreclosed where it serves our national interests." [24] Potential stresses and strains might be lessened and their political repercussions dulled if the grants were channeled through an international agency or a consortium whose guiding principles had been negotiated by developed and underdeveloped countries alike.

Which Form of Financing for Which Activities?

Logically, agreement on a country's estimated total requirements for hard loans, soft loans, and grants during a 3- to 5-year period

[24] *Third Interim Report of the President's Committee to Study the United States Military Assistance Program* (Draper Committee), July 13, 1959, p. 41. See also Mason Report, pp. 9-10: ". . . Foreign assistance was not instituted primarily to achieve economic gain for the United States but as an instrument for the achievement of U.S. foreign policy objectives. Those programs which generate local currency were not originated with the objective of collecting local currency but with the political and security interests of the United States as their goal. Therefore, the test of value received—the test of whether such programs are really a 'giveaway'—is not whether an equivalent amount of money accrues to the United States in repayment for its assistance but whether our basic foreign policy objectives are, in fact, achieved. That this cannot be measured until considerable time has elapsed, and therefore may be difficult for the public to understand, does not alter the fact that this is the only valid yardstick."

should precede the securing of foreign public financing for specific projects. Under this order of business, it would be easier to ascertain whether the proposed projects represented priority undertakings within the agreed program and whether the total amount provided in the form of loans and grants for specific projects added up to the amount of foreign public financing needed for the overall program. Historically, funds have been made available to finance specific development projects with little reference to any systematic calculation of anticipated program deficits. One of the prime tasks of policy today is to bring logic and history into closer consonance: to facilitate realization of over-all development programs while associating a major portion of the available foreign assistance with identifiable undertakings within those programs.

The identity of the undertakings financed by foreign loan and by foreign grant will not matter greatly so long as repayment prospects are assessed in terms of the economy as a whole. The decision can be based on convenience—on the character of the projects with which the aid-giver wishes to identify itself, on the commodities it can most readily supply, on the skills of the people it can make available for participation in the program, on the activities least likely to be financed by private investment.

The evolution of foreign aid since the end of the Marshall Plan has produced a much more disorganized patchwork. A hallmark of the last half dozen years, mentioned in Chapter 3, has been the proliferation of sources of aid. All except the International Cooperation Administration concentrate on project assistance only, and each agency is limited by legal and administrative restrictions concerning the types of projects it can finance. The definition of what constitutes a project has undergone steady expansion, but no agency or combination of agencies is responsible for providing project assistance and supplementary resources sufficient to meet the agreed national objectives of the developing country. Practices that make the matching of project assistance and program requirements extremely difficult have over time acquired the dignity of principles.

It may be politically awkward, for example, to provide aid for competitive undertakings, but it should be recognized that the very process of economic development means making the developing nation more competitive in almost every field for which it has real potentialities. Refusal to give aid for textile plants or cotton production or state-owned industries may have adverse political effects in the developing country but will have no economic consequences if the country has other resources which can be applied to the undertaking. The adverse effects may become economic as well as political if the country is prevented by law from assigning United States resources, and discouraged in practice from using its own resources, for such purposes.[25]

Questionable also is the view that foreign investment should be concentrated on projects that will increase the country's exports or decrease its imports.

> It is futile to earmark foreign investment for the export-import industries and domestic investment for purely home industries.
>
> Every foreign investment, like every domestic investment, is consistent with a strong balance of payments, provided the investment is in response to a market demand for the output and does not give rise to inflation. The only important principle for guiding the direction of investment is that it should be in industries for which the economy is suited.[26]

Giving greater attention to the potentiality of the underdeveloped economy as a whole might give rise in addition to some second thoughts on interest rate policy. Interest rates charged by the Development Loan Fund, for example, are based on the type of project financed:

> ... If the activity is classed as economic overhead (including roads, ports, etc.) a rate approximating the current cost of money to the U.S. Government is used. Currently the rate for this type of project is 3½%.

---

[25] Relevant legal provisions include the Cooley amendment, Section 104(e), of P.L. 480, authorizing the setting aside of a portion of the local currency proceeds of sales of agricultural products for loans to private enterprise. It prohibits such loans for the manufacture of products to be exported to the United States in competition with products produced in the United States, or for the manufacture or production of commodities "to be marketed in competition with United States agricultural commodities or the products thereof." The Mutual Security Act of 1954, as amended June 30, 1958, Sections 202(b) and 413(c), requires the Development Loan Fund to take into account "possible adverse effects upon the economy of the United States," and gives similar instructions to the International Cooperation Administration.

[26] *Economic Development With Stability*, a Report to the Government of India by a Mission of the International Monetary Fund (1953), p. 72.

For profit-making types of projects the DLF normally charges a rate comparable to that charged by the Export-Import Bank. At the present time this rate is about 5¾%.[27]

Most DLF loans are repayable in local currencies, fundamentally because of doubt about the wisdom of saddling the borrowing nation with a formal obligation to repay in real resources. In view of doubt about its ability to repay the principal, it is perhaps odd, from the United States point of view, that any interest at all is demanded. The reason may be that the United States attaches little importance to the pyramiding of its local currency claims through interest accumulations, but wishes to foster necessary financial discipline within the borrowing country.

To do this, it is not essential that the United States set the terms governing access to capital by profit-making and nonprofit-making ventures *within* the borrowing countries. Our primary concern is the terms on which resources are made available *to* the borrowing countries. The terms on which the borrowing government wishes them to be made available for internal use is a separable issue, which can be decided on the basis of its national needs and other domestic considerations.

The collection of interest on loans repayable in local currency may serve only to swell a United States account that is already excessive. On the other hand, the use of either United States-owned local currency or counterpart funds for debt reduction in foreign countries has been forbidden by law since 1953. Attempts to remove the prohibition have been unsuccessful. Experts are convinced, however, that the use of United States local currency balances for purposes of debt retirement is frequently the most constructive action possible.[28]

From its inception, technical assistance has been provided almost entirely on a grant basis, free of requirements concerning counter-

---

[27] Development Loan Fund, *Fiscal Year 1960 Estimates*, p. 15. The summary continues with the statement: "Particularly in those cases where DLF funds are reloaned by intermediaries to local private borrowers, as in the case of loans to development banks, exceptions to this general rate policy have been necessary in order to allow for reasonable charges by the secondary lender and a reasonable rate to the ultimate borrower."

[28] Mason Report, pp. 15 and 28.

part deposits, and there appears to be no disposition to change the system. Since the cost of foreign experts, teachers, and fellowships is one of the smallest costs of a development program, there is no strong economic reason for sparing the developing countries this modest burden. By the same token, there is no great economic advantage in transferring it to them. More important is the need for a close relationship between technical assistance and capital assistance projects, and the difficulty of obtaining necessary coordination so long as both the capital-providing agencies—the DLF, the Export-Import Bank, the International Bank, the Inter-American Development Bank, the International Development Association, etc.—and the purveyors of technical assistance—the International Cooperation Administration, the United Nations and its specialized agencies, the United Nations Special Fund, and others—remain relatively autonomous.

Only when the situation reaches crisis proportions, as it recently has in India, in Spain, in Argentina, and in one or two other areas, do the "independent" aid-giving agencies manage to get together and offer a collective life-line to the sinking swimmer. In such cases, the International Monetary Fund and private banks have been associated in the rescue operation. To date, an economic crisis has been a necessary forerunner of real coordination of foreign aid efforts, but the apparent success of the consortium approach, where it has been applied, suggests the desirability of employing the technique at an earlier stage.

The essence of the technique is simple. Under the leadership of the International Bank or some equally respected auspices, and in the company of informed representatives of the country in need of foreign aid, representatives of the major sources of aid reappraise requirements and agree on a division of labor for meeting those requirements. Each agency provides the type of project or other aid that it is legally authorized and administratively equipped to provide. The total minimum requirements of the receiving country for short- and longer-term assistance in grant and loan form become known, however, and, within these limits, project decisions can be based on mutual convenience.[29]

[29] ". . . If these consortia are to serve development over the long run, they must not be regarded primarily as a fund-raising exercise or as a means of

Unless some such system is institutionalized—and soon—further fragmentation is inevitable. The number of countries offering foreign aid and the number seeking foreign aid are both on the increase. Regional banks and funds are springing up to supplement the existing array of national and international institutions. The underdeveloped countries, though they occasionally benefit from increased competition among donors, are usually too weak to take advantage of the situation. They have already tied up more talent than they can spare in vain efforts to learn what is available from whom, how to qualify for it, and how to eke out a program from it.

Translating Country Requirements into Global Requirements

If the major underdeveloped countries were committed to the preparation of development programs from which their separate requirements for foreign aid could be estimated roughly, what standards could be used for appraising those requirements, what would the individual totals add up to, and how would the totals compare with the amounts currently being received?

If the techniques discussed in the preceding portions of this chapter were utilized, the desirable rate of development would be defined in terms of a rate of increase in national income such as 6 per cent per year. The amount of investment required to achieve the agreed percentage increase in each country would be estimated. Some countries might be able to raise the full amount from their own resources plus private foreign investment, but in most cases there would be a gap between the sum needed and the sum that could be raised. This gap would represent foreign aid requirements at their maximum. If the country failed to mobilize domestic

---

securing temporary accommodations in political and economic crises. The need is not just for finance, but for efficient and effective development programming. If international cooperation is really to serve the desired objective, it must encourage the orderly programming of projects and resources, primarily by the recipient country itself. Where this vital condition is met, these credit consortia can provide further convincing evidence of the worth of the international approach." W. A. B. Iliff, Vice President of the International Bank, address to Bank and Fund meetings, *International Financial News Survey*, Sept. 30, 1960, p. 520.

resources in accordance with its potentialities, foreign aid would be scaled down proportionately. The aid made available would take the form of loans to the extent permitted by the debt-servicing capacity of the country. Grant aid would not be excluded on grounds of principle, however.

So summarized, the procedure inevitably sounds more mechanical and arbitrary than it could possibly be in practice. It is vulnerable from many standpoints. Underwriting different rates of increase in per capita income in different countries may be hard to justify. Distributing aid—

> to achieve *equal percentage growth* of income per capita among countries . . . would probably tend to provide more aid to higher-income countries than if equal shares of aid per capita were provided, since it would yield them larger absolute increases in total production through equal percentages; it would also require relatively less aid for the countries most capable of rapid growth.[30]

There is no assurance that aid allocations based on equal percentage increases in income would permit necessary progress toward another goal of development programs—productive employment for those able and willing to work. Moreover, at what per capita level of income should a country be judged capable of mobilizing independently the resources required for self-sustaining growth? Should countries with per capita incomes in excess of $300 per year at 1960 prices be eligible for development assistance other than, for example, hard loans?

Universally applicable criteria for objectively evaluating foreign aid requirements will not emerge in the foreseeable future. Each country will still have to be treated in large measure as a special case, and experimentation in the planning and execution of development programs should be encouraged.

Fortunately, objective, universally applicable criteria for evaluating aid requirements are not prerequisites for attaining a measure of consensus; witness the experience of the Marshall Plan countries

---

[30] Schelling, *International Economics*, p. 460. See pp. 459ff. for comments on other criteria for measuring need.

and, more recently, the widespread agreement on the needs of India and Pakistan. Consideration of country programs at a regional or other higher level can lead to estimates less subjective and better understood than those currently serving as bases for development assistance. The initial purpose of an international analysis would be to note and evaluate the broad goals of each program and the assumptions made concerning domestic investment and savings, private foreign investment, world market prices for internationally traded commodities, population trends, internal distribution of anticipated increases in the gross national product, and other key items. Out of these analyses should come better projections than are presently available of the amount of outside aid needed individually and collectively by the underdeveloped countries of the free world in order to permit gradual, broadly diffused improvements in local levels of living, without resort to Draconian measures, without excessive centralization of decision-making, and with real effort on the part of each country concerned.

At different times during the past decade attempts have been made to estimate requirements on a global basis. In the absence of realistic country programs or adequate background statistics on which to base projections, these estimates have been quite crude. The first widely publicized estimates were released in May 1951 by a group of five experts appointed by the United Nations Secretary-General to prepare recommendations for the Economic and Social Council on the economic development of underdeveloped countries. They introduced their calculations of requirements for external capital with caveats which have become standard:

> . . . This is clearly a very difficult question to answer. It involves making very hazardous guesses as to their present national incomes, their rates of population increase, and the cost and productivity of different types of investment. Since statistical information about most of these countries is very scanty, the limits of error are at best very wide. In the circumstances, we have debated at some length whether it would serve any useful purpose to suggest any figures in this sphere, and whether we should not merely leave the matter by saying that these countries will pro-

gress faster if they get more capital, and more slowly if they get less.[31]

The experts concluded that a 2 per cent increase in per capita national income would require an annual capital import into the underdeveloped countries "well in excess of $10 billion" for investment in industry and agriculture alone.[32] They painted with broad strokes and included little evidence of the ability of underdeveloped countries to make effective use of capital in the amounts indicated. A 1957 publication by two well-known American economists laid much greater stress on the concept of absorptive capacity:

> Thus, if all countries were equally efficient at working out acceptable national programs and projects, a commitment made today of a target amount of annual aid should lead to disbursements beginning on a large scale only after about three years. If by this process absorptive capacity were increased by 30-50 per cent, the amount of foreign investment called for would be, at a maximum, about 3.5 billion per annum. This amount would make possible a rise in per capita output of at least 1 or 2 per cent per year. Technical absorptive capacity would continue to rise after the first three years by 5 to 10 per cent per year, but the additional capital required to take advantage of this rise could be supplied from domestic savings.
>
> In practice, the rate at which countries will be able to qualify for capital will vary according to their stage of development. . . . it seems most unlikely that, if a commitment to make available 3.5 billion dollars annually is entered into, the rate of actual disbursement will rise above, say, 60 per cent of that amount. . . . The 3.5 billion dollar figure is in addition to what is now flowing.[33]

The figures submitted for illustrative purposes to the Senate Foreign Relations Committee in November 1959 by the Maxwell Graduate School of Citizenship and Public Affairs at Syracuse University were closer to the original estimates by the United Nations experts. The total amount of foreign capital being made available

---

[31] United Nations Secretariat, Department of Economic Affairs, *Measures for the Economic Development of Under-Developed Countries,* Report by a Group of Experts Appointed by the Secretary-General of the United Nations, May 1951, p. 75.

[32] *Ibid.,* p. 79.

[33] Max F. Millikan and W. W. Rostow, *A Proposal, Key to an Effective Foreign Policy* (Harper & Bros., 1957), pp. 102-03.

to the underdeveloped areas of the free world was roughly and rather generously estimated to be about $5 billion in 1959 and the capital deficit to be between $5 and $10 billion.

Could the underdeveloped areas of the free world utilize an additional $10 billion in foreign capital a year, if the advanced countries were to make this sum available? The answer, of course, must be "No." If the funds were to be used for consumption goods, this and much larger sums could be used, providing the consumption goods could be produced in the necessary quantities. But in capital goods, this additional amount of money could not be transferred into physical products without a huge increase in waste and misuse, in price increases and nonessential expenditures. The factor which most limits absorptive capacity is unquestionably the time it takes in an underdeveloped country to train the kinds of specialists and administrators and build the kinds of social institutions (schools, banks, factory organizations, health services, experiment stations, Government agencies, and so on) required to get the modernization process under way.

. . . A rough guess, in which some sort of consensus could probably be secured is that at least $3 billion or $4 billion of additional capital could be utilized each year by the less-developed areas, and that the amount that could annually be absorbed will increase over the next 10 years. This additional capital, while not sufficient to increase per capita gross national product by 2 per cent, would be sufficient to make a marked increase in the rate of growth; progress would be visible where at present, in most of the less-developed countries, it is alarmingly difficult to detect.[34]

Although the assumptions of Paul Hoffman, Managing Director of the United Nations Special Fund, concerning national income in the underdeveloped countries today and present levels of foreign investment in those countries differ from those of the Maxwell School, his conclusions are consistent with theirs. He believes that to increase the growth in per capita income in underdeveloped countries from an average of 1 per cent per year in the 1950's to an average of 2 per cent in the 1960's, about $3 billion per year— $30 billion in a decade—over and above present levels will be needed from outside sources. Of this $30 billion, some $10 billion

---

[34] *The Operational Aspects of United States Foreign Policy*, a Study Prepared at the Request of the Senate Committee on Foreign Relations, Nov. 11, 1959, p. 43.

will be covered by increases in private investment and "through increases in existing bilateral and multilateral aid and investment programs (e.g., the Development Loan Fund). This leaves something on the order of $20 billion which has to be found, during the 1960's, from sources which are at present not available." [35]

Meeting Global Requirements

In every year since the close of World War II, the United States has devoted some of its resources to economic development abroad. Others among the so-called developed countries, as they have recovered from the damage and destruction of the war, have enlarged their foreign aid programs. The combined efforts of the more industrialized nations do not yet add up to the best available estimates of requirements. Moreover, the burden—or privilege—of aiding the underdeveloped countries appears to be haphazardly if not inequitably shared by the more fortunate nations. The need for criteria to govern burden-sharing is therefore great, but an adequate discussion of potential criteria is beyond the scope of this publication.

Major educational efforts will be required to convince the voters and parliaments of the more developed countries of the desirability of providing resources in a coordinated manner, on the scale required, for as many years to come as necessary. It is perhaps difficult at present to envisage development programs for 50 or more low-income countries being prepared and reviewed from the standpoint of feasibility and actual performance, with some 20 higher-income countries sharing equitably the burden of meeting agreed program deficits. Moreover, unless the Soviet Union can be associated in the exercise, its independent incursions into development financing will have to be taken into account—in much the same *post facto* fashion as variations in the flow of private capital, sudden changes in export prices, or unexpected capital/output ratios.

For the United States, additional complications may arise because evenly paced economic development is not the only interest we may

[35] Hoffman, *op. cit.*, p. 46. See also similar estimates in *Goals for Americans*, the Report of the President's Commission on National Goals (Prentice-Hall, Inc., 1960), pp. 17 and 345.

have in a given underdeveloped area. For some time to come, situations—political, military, or economic—may arise in which the United States will wish to treat some countries differently from others. In such cases, the most sensible course will be to admit frankly that we have military alliances, political interests, and regional loyalties requiring us to do more than meet internationally agreed development goals. We will then have to participate, on a case-by-case basis, in the supplementary programs that appear to be needed, in such fashion as to achieve maximum progress toward our multiple objectives in the area. At the same time it would be wise to recognize that in aid, as in trade, discriminatory treatment has serious long-run disadvantages and the ultimate goal should be equitable treatment for all those prepared to observe established ground rules.

5

Summary and Conclusions

BECAUSE NEITHER PRACTICE nor theory is well understood, the grant/loan controversy has been vastly oversimplified. Public discussion of the pros and cons of different techniques of financing foreign aid has been too largely in moral terms. Grant aid for economic development, it is widely believed, is inherently bad; loan aid, however soft, is preferable. On the other hand, the extension of military aid, technical assistance, and famine relief on a grant basis is right and proper. Decisions have been reached without adequate analysis of the debt-servicing capacities of aid-receiving countries or of the rate and type of growth most likely to promote the general welfare.

Greater awareness is needed of precisely how grant aid differs from loan aid, how hard loans differ from soft loans, and how sales of surplus commodities for local currencies differ from sales for dollars. Such knowledge is a prerequisite for arrival at balanced judgments of whether the objectives of aid programs can be achieved by exclusive reliance on any particular form of financing. If various forms of financing are needed, how should the combination be determined? Although every effort has been made in this study to present problems in a manner that permits the reader to reach his own independent conclusions, it may be useful to summarize or to repeat here the main findings and conclusions that seem to the author to emerge from this study.

Through aid programs, foreign countries become able to import "essential" equipment, supplies, and services over and above what they would obtain in the normal course of trade, or as a result of private investment, private remittances, and the expenditures of

American tourists during the period in question. There is, however, no necessary connection between the financial terms on which the United States makes the aid available to a foreign country and the financial terms on which such aid subsequently becomes available to business enterprises and private citizens in the country aided. The government receiving aid can sell at prevailing prices the commodities that it has received on a grant basis. It can give away commodities for which it has had to pay. It can use either grant or loan aid, or both, to establish a lending institution within its boundaries which makes loans at rates of interest higher or lower than the cost of the capital obtained from abroad.

The purposes to be served by the funds appropriated for foreign aid have changed radically since 1945. The promotion of economic growth and political stability in the less developed regions of the world has gradually become the central objective of foreign assistance policy. The course that should be followed to reach that objective is far from obvious, however, and sharp differences of opinion have been expressed concerning costs and methods of financing the journey.

Volume and Distribution of Aid

Through its major and minor programs, the United States Government during the 15½ years between July 1, 1945, and December 31, 1960, provided net foreign grants and credits valued at about $75 billion. Because of various exclusions—among them, the investment of the United States in certain international institutions—this total may understate by about $7 billion what is frequently referred to as "the burden of foreign aid on the already heavily burdened American taxpayer." On the other hand, the inclusion of expenditures that would almost certainly have been made by the Government for military equipment and agricultural commodities, even if there were no foreign aid programs, probably inflates the burden by $10 to $20 billion.

The big postwar programs have been grant programs; net grants constitute more than 85 per cent of net grants and credits utilized since mid-1945. Net grants represent the difference between gross grants made by the United States and reverse grants and returns received by the United States from abroad. Net credits represent the difference between new loans and principal collections on outstanding loans. Repayments of principal have tripled since 1950 and serve as a substantial offset to new credits. Total principal repayments since mid-1945 amount to approximately $7 billion.

Next to Western Europe, Asia, with net grants and credits in excess of $22 billion by the close of 1960, has been by far the largest receiver of United States aid. Less than 4 per cent of the net grants and credits extended by the United States Government during the postwar period has gone to Latin America, and public assistance to this region, more than to any other, has taken the form of loans. Principal collections from Latin America have been larger than United States aid to Africa, last of the great continents to awaken to the revolution of rising expectations.

In 1959, the burden of foreign grants and credits on the American economy, as indicated by the ratio of foreign aid expenditures to gross national product, was less than one third of what it had been in 1946—down from 2.5 per cent to 0.8 per cent. Most of the aid funds have been spent on goods and services of American origin. The increased deficits in the United States balance of payments during 1958-60 cannot to any significant extent be attributed to our foreign aid expenditures, which were lower in total and more concentrated in the United States during those years than during any other three years of the last decade.

Aid which successfully promotes growth and development abroad will, of course, gradually enlarge the production base and the export potential of the receiving countries, thereby improving their competitive position in world markets and reducing their need for certain imports. Attempts to prevent or discourage investment in activities competitive with United States output are contrary to the basic purposes of development assistance, unless the economy of the foreign country is equally well adapted to an alternative, less-competitive form of production. Investments, domestic and foreign, should be channeled into those activities for which the economies of the countries receiving assistance are best suited, regardless of short-run effects on the foreign trade of the United States.

To finance nonmilitary foreign aid, the United States, during the last few years, has relied increasingly on loan assistance. New credits now represent close to 40 per cent of new economic and technical aid. Some of these credits continue to take the form of "hard" loans repayable in dollars within 15 to 25 years. More are taking the form of "soft" loans repayable over still longer periods of time in the currency of the borrowing country—in rupees, hwan, or piastres. Numerous problems have arisen as a result of aid programs that generate local currencies and require them to be placed in earmarked accounts.

Local Currency Problems

When the United States provides as grant aid commodities other than military supplies and equipment, the receiving government is required to deposit in a counterpart account the local currency proceeds which it derives from selling the commodities to its own nationals. With certain exceptions, such as construction equipment retained by ministries of public works or DDT used by public health services for malaria control, nonmilitary, aid-financed commodities are disposed of through normal channels of trade. Purchasers pay for them in the currency of their land; they do not receive them as gifts. The resultant counterpart account is owned by the country receiving the aid. A small portion (commonly referred to as "10 per cent counterpart") is normally turned over to the United States for such uses as paying the local expenses of American embassies, missions, and traveling Congressmen. To this extent, the recipient country makes a partial repayment for grant aid.

The balance of the counterpart (90 per cent counterpart) remains in the possession of the depositing country, but is available solely for expenditures agreed to by the United States. The United States can veto proposed expenditures of counterpart funds, but foreign governments can, if they wish, circumvent the veto by printing additional quantities of their own currency or by using the deposit as an additional basis for the extension of credit. The United States cannot compel foreign governments to spend counterpart if they do not desire to do so.

Unlike counterpart funds which are owned by the countries that receive grant aid, Public Law 480 local currencies—local currencies resulting from the sale of surplus agricultural products pursuant to Title I of the Agricultural Trade Development and Assistance Act —are owned by the United States Government. Although dollar payment could not reasonably be expected, giving the commodities away has been assumed to be politically unacceptable in the United States, save in cases of famine relief and analagous emergencies. The compromise solution has been to "sell" some $5 billion worth of commodities for inconvertible currencies that "belong" to the United States. At least 10 per cent of the sales proceeds is reserved for United States Government use, whether needed or not, and another fraction (up to 25 per cent) is reserved for loans to private enterprise under the Cooley amendment to P.L. 480. Most of the remainder is used for loans and grants to the country that made the purchase.

P.L. 480 sales at present represent by far the largest, but not the sole, source of United States-owned local currency accumulations. Other sources include the so-called program loans of the International Cooperation Administration and the lending activity of the Development Loan Fund. The latter agency is authorized to accept foreign currencies in repayment of its dollar loans and to use the repayments for additional lending. As a result of interest charges to borrowers plus interest earned on undisbursed portions of United States-owned local currency accounts in foreign banks, the amount of local currency held by the United States can ultimately exceed by a considerable sum the amount originally received from sales of surplus commodities and loans of dollar exchange.

Both foreign-owned counterpart funds and United States-owned local currency accounts are built up as a result of agreements with countries that receive from the United States a real resource of immediate value—agricultural commodities or other goods. To the extent that the accounts are drawn down by the United States for its own administrative expenses or for other uses that would ordinarily require dollar expenditures, the United States obtains payment in real terms. With respect to the balance, it expects no further direct return from the foreign-owned counterpart fund.

The financial return from the remainder of the United States-owned local currency accounts depends on the extent to which they are ultimately converted into goods and services of value to the United States.

The differences between foreign-owned counterpart funds and United States-owned local currency accounts are more important legally and politically than economically. Neither can command additional imports; neither serves as a substitute for dollar aid. A foreign government, however, is more likely to grow uneasy about the American-owned account, fearful that substantial accumulations of its currency in the hands of foreigners may give outsiders a means of frustrating its monetary or its development policies. It has been pointed out, for example, that American holdings of Indian rupees may easily approach the equivalent of $2.5 billion by 1963. "Now $2.5 billion in relation to the Indian national income is roughly equivalent to $35 billion in this country. Imagine the reaction in the United States if a foreign country, no matter how friendly, held $35 billion in our currency."[1]

The American-owned account is also the greater potential source of confusion in the United States. To prove that they are selling and lending, not granting, the Department of Agriculture and the Development Loan Fund tend to exaggerate the usefulness of the local currency deposits acquired as a result of their activities. These agencies, plus the Treasury and the Bureau of the Budget, have typically been uneasy about proposals to make grants from such deposits. To prevent the Congress from cutting its dollar appropriations, the International Cooperation Administration, on the other hand, is compelled to stress the limited value of inconvertible foreign currency as a United States asset and disposed to favor grants as a means of precluding or reducing embarrassing accumulations.

In six or eight key countries, even the fraction of local currency accounts reserved to date for United States uses exceeds the foreseeable requirements of our government for many years to come.

[1] Edward S. Mason, "Foreign Money We Can't Spend," *Atlantic Monthly*, May 1960, p. 81.

While this situation prevails, the acquisition of additional 10 per cent and 25 per cent shares of the proceeds of future sales should be unnecessary, and steps to scale down present holdings should be taken.

Additional policy changes are needed to prevent excessive accumulations because of interest payments and principal repayments on (a) loans from the country-use portion of the proceeds of local currency sales, and (b) dollar loans repayable in local currency. Such measures might include repealing the legal prohibitions against using local currency accounts for debt retirement in the foreign country; establishing binational foundations which would invest in government securities in the host country part of the currency given to them from United States holdings; lowering interest rates and eliminating maintenance-of-value provisions in certain instances; and making more grants, *ab initio,* of our surplus commodities.[2]

To adopt policies that will hold down American accumulations of foreign currencies to sums that can be repaid to the United States in real resources raises the much larger question of how requirements for hard loans, soft loans, and grants can be estimated.

Realities of Foreign Grants and Loans

Whether aid takes the form of a hard loan, a soft loan, or a grant makes very little difference to the firm supplying the aid-financed goods. The American producer expects to be paid in dollars and is so paid for items exported under foreign aid programs. Similarly, the end-user in the receiving country normally pays the going price in local currency for what he gets. American exporter and foreign importer can usually deal directly with each other. The purchaser has all the customary incentives to buy only what he needs and in the process to expend the minimum amount of local currency. The seller has all the customary incentives to

[2] *The Problem of Excess Accumulation of U.S.-Owned Local Currencies,* Findings and Recommendations Submitted to the Under Secretary of State by the Consultants on International Finance and Economic Problems, Apr. 4, 1960 (Mason Report), *passim.*

dispose profitably of his wares and thus to obtain the dollars needed to remain in business.

If the consumer in the receiving country pays the going price for what he gets, in the only currency in which he can deal, it is difficult to see how he, as an individual, can be demoralized by foreign aid. Insofar as he is concerned, there has been no giveaway, no soft loan, no significant deviation from normal commercial practices.

Although the individual citizen is not a direct beneficiary, he belongs to a community that benefits. Collectively, the citizens of the receiving country gain to the extent that they receive useful goods and services from abroad without having to export goods and services of comparable value. In a more technical sense, the beneficiary is usually their government. If the imports come as grant aid and are sold within the country, the foreign government will have, in a counterpart fund, local currency which it did not have to raise by taxation or by borrowing. If the imports take the form of grants of capital goods or consumer goods retained by the receiving government, its own inventory of physical equipment will be swelled. If the imports are financed by a loan repayable in local currency, the foreign government may have access, through reborrowing, to the deposits it makes in the United States-owned account. If the imports are financed by a loan repayable in dollars, the government may have the use of local currency derived from the sale of the goods until it has to release the equivalent in foreign exchange.

The possibility of drawing on an account that does not have to be raised by taxation or by borrowing from its own citizenry could be demoralizing to a government in the sense of relaxing pressures for frugality and the most careful husbanding of resources. The built-in protection against inefficient use of these resources is the requirement for United States concurrence with respect to expenditures from counterpart and local currency accounts. The theory is that consultation will result in expenditures more favorable to economic recovery, stability, development, or defense than would otherwise have been the case. The decision that is negotiated, however, may be worse, not better, than it would have been in the absence of consultation, or it may be better but not good enough to qualify the government as a competent manager of the resources at its disposal.

Projects and Programs

For the most part, foreign grants and credits are earmarked for designated power plants, highways, and educational institutions, on the theory that allocations to specific projects ensure a better use of resources than the same sums made available for a nation-wide development or reconstruction program without such earmarking. There have been lively debates over what constitutes a project. With the acceptance of the establishment of national development banks, training institutes, land-improvement programs, and similar activities as projects, the concept has gradually been broadened. Further broadening, in order to remove some of the remaining ambiguities surrounding the project concept, would be desirable. Nonproject aid will nevertheless continue to be needed in order to provide imported repair and maintenance materials, consumer goods, and other items not readily allocable to specific projects.

At present, the International Cooperation Administration is the only member of the ever-lengthening list of agencies providing foreign grants and credits that can be described as program-oriented, and the description even in this instance would be more courtesy than fact. To prepare what it terms "country programs," the ICA engages in an elaborate, time-consuming exercise, the upshot of which is not a comprehensive long-range investment program designed to facilitate orderly progress toward some agreed goals, but a bulky aide-mémoire in support of its annual appropriation request to the United States Congress.

Estimating Requirements

Country requirements for development aid can be estimated by a number of methods, none of which can be described as scientific, objective, or free of political judgments. This writer agrees that the need for outside assistance depends on the rate of development considered desirable and the extent to which a country can reach that rate by mobilizing and utilizing its own resources. He also agrees that, although there is no single criterion of a desirable rate of development, there is much to be said in favor of defining it in terms of a rate of increase in national income, such as 6 per cent per year. Then the smaller the population increase, the greater will be the increase in income per capita.

The amount of investment required to achieve the agreed goals in each country can be estimated. Some underdeveloped countries might be able to raise the full amount from their own resources, but in most cases there would be a gap between the sum needed and the sum that could be raised. The gap would represent foreign aid requirements at their maximum. If the country failed to mobilize available resources in accordance with its potentialities, foreign aid should be scaled down proportionately.

Loan Requirements

How should the requirement for foreign aid be divided among hard loans, soft loans, and grants? The amount of foreign debt that can be serviced by an economy undergoing profound structural change can be forecast only within a wide range. The lower end of the range—AX in the chart on page 96—would represent the consensus of conservative estimates of the country's growth and export earnings. The upper end of the range, which might be 25 to 30 per cent higher and extends from X to Y on the chart, would represent a consensus based on more optimistic assumptions.

While foreign indebtedness remains below "X," the chances of repayment on schedule are good. "X" therefore marks a probable upper limit for lending activity by what might be thought of as the holders of first mortgages, i.e., private bondholders and public lending institutions such as the World Bank and the Export-Import Bank. The second mortgage holders—institutions such as the Development Loan Fund and the International Development Association that are prepared to take some risks beyond those customarily assumed by the conventional lending agencies—should concentrate their efforts in the area between X and Y. The country's estimated total need for foreign capital in order to increase its national income by an agreed percentage per year might extend still higher, to point Z. The difference between Z and Y would then represent the need for grant aid.

The conventional lending agencies would continue to expect to be repaid in full. Failure of a debtor country to service its outstanding loans would inevitably classify the country as in default of its international obligations and probably disqualify it from further borrowing from those agencies until it had agreed on settlement terms for its unpaid outstanding indebtedness.

In the Y minus X range, where debt-servicing ability would depend on progress more rapid than the custodians of revolving funds can safely count on, inability to repay on schedule should not classify the borrower as a defaulter on its international obligations. Making loans in the Y minus X range repayable in the currency of the borrower is a convenient way of distinguishing them from other foreign debt and postponing releases of equivalent amounts of foreign exchange during the early years of a development program. Such action would be consistent with the practices of the Development Loan Fund but contrary to the present intentions of the International Development Association.

The IDA intends to make its loans in dollars, pounds, francs, and marks, as the International Bank does, but on easier terms. This will enable developing countries to increase the debt load that they can carry, because the annual payments due on a 40-year, 2½ per cent loan of $100 million or any other sum will be considerably smaller than those due on a 20-year loan of the same amount at 5 per cent interest. The disadvantage is that there will still be a tendency to hold the total debt burden down to the amount that can be serviced on rather conservative estimates of the country's development potential. In the view of this writer, it would be preferable to permit a total debt burden based on more liberal assumptions, with the intermediate area reserved for a special type of lending with which the world is gradually becoming familiar, the loan repayable in local currency. At the same time, it must be recognized that, if the latter is really a loan, it will ultimately have to be repaid in real resources by foregoing goods and services that might otherwise be consumed or invested at home.

Current procedures for determining the volume of lending on

easier terms than those of the conventional lending agencies bear little resemblance to the procedure outlined above. The probability that the borrowing country will eventually be able to release enough foreign exchange to repay in real resources its accumulated P. L. 480, DLF, and other local currency loans is rarely assessed with care.

Full repayment in foreign exchange is likely to be the exception rather than the rule. When some of our local currency holdings have to be written off, the American people, not having been adequately prepared for this eventuality, may feel deceived. Meanwhile, foreign countries may have grown excessively uneasy about the amount of their currency piling up in United States or other alien hands—far more uneasy than if they had known all along that the upper limits for such holdings had been calculated with the prospects for conversion into foreign exchange clearly in mind.

If the final settlement takes the form of granting some of the United States-owned local currency to the developing country, it may be difficult for the American people to understand that the commodities that gave rise to the United States-owned accumulation will long ago have been consumed, and the receiving country will not be enriched in any real sense by acquiring title to an additional quantity of its own currency.

Grant Requirements

Giving back to the buyer the currency with which he bought the commodities in the first place is only a roundabout way of giving him the commodities. It makes little sense to close the front door to grant aid for economic development, as the Congress has been doing, while leaving open the back door and several trap doors— namely, grants of local currency acquired through "sales" of such commodities or grants of surplus commodities by nongovernmental relief and welfare agencies that obtained the commodities from governmental agencies.

Analyses of investment requirements and of debt-servicing capacity would probably show that tolerable rates of economic progress in some free-world countries could not be made on the basis of mobilizable domestic resources, private foreign investment, and public loans from abroad, including local currency loans up to the limits for which there were reasonable prospects of repayment in real terms. These countries would be candidates for grant aid. India, Pakistan, Vietnam, Burma, Haiti, Bolivia, and some of the newly independent countries of Africa would be among them.

While it is clear that the possibilities of further international lending of the kind engaged in by the World Bank are by no means exhausted, it is also apparent that the debt-servicing burden in some of the underdeveloped countries has risen sharply. In several Latin American countries, other than those mentioned above, service payments on public debt alone have been taking more than 10 per cent of earnings from abroad. In India more than $1 billion will be required for the repayment of external debt during the period covered by the Third Five Year Plan. Because of this obligation, foreign aid requirements will be nearly 25 per cent greater than the $4.4 billion believed necessary for net imports during 1961-65.

If grant aid for economic development is not available, the alternative for the low-income countries is to scale down their development programs below the "desirable" rate or to seek to extract larger savings from a population already at the margin of subsistence. Either course may jeopardize the progress toward democratic institutions which is, and should be, a major objective of American involvement in foreign aid programs.

The procedure proposed herein implies a program as well as a project approach to the promotion of economic growth in the less developed regions. A country, alone or in collaboration with others, establishes its targets or economic goals and frames a medium- or longer-term program—a 3-, 4-, 5-, or 10-year plan—for reaching those goals. Foreign sources of financial assistance should be equipped to review constructively the proposed country development program or, if the area does not yet have a program, to help prepare one that is realistic in relation to the potentialities of that country and consistent with the plans of other friendly countries. To ensure that trained and literate personnel become available in sufficient numbers, and to help assess requirements for technical as well as financial assistance, educational and training programs must be prepared along with investment programs. Periodic reviews of progress toward agreed goals should be made, not only domestically, but also at some international level. The quality of investment is every bit as important as the quantity.

Concluding Caveats

Summarized as it has been here, the whole procedure sounds more rigid than it could possibly be in practice. In the absence of any generally accepted theory or strategy of economic and political development, there can be no single blueprint for progress. The programming exercise suggested here is vulnerable from many standpoints; wide latitude must therefore be given for experimentation and adjustment.

The preparation of a development program involves judgments on many matters that far transcend the realm of economics: the requirements for national defense, the allocation of resources between consumption and investment, the probable effects of policy decisions on personal habits and motivations. The judgments reached will vary from country to country and will affect requirements for foreign aid. All the estimates and projections in development programming are subject, in any event, to considerable margins of error, with the estimates of requirements for grant aid subject to wider margins than any of the other figures.

Nevertheless, the programming exercise should give countries a recurring sense of purpose, pace, and direction, and a series of focal points around which latent energies can be galvanized. Programming is not a *sine qua non* of progress, but a nation made aware of the size and nature of the problems facing it is at least as likely to address itself to the important ones as a nation that fails to look before it leaps—or fails to leap because it has not looked.

The growing consensus about the requirements of India and Pakistan indicates that analyses and projections which will generally be regarded as reasonable can be made. Over time, it should be possible to make similar estimates for other nations and, in fact, progressively to refine the whole process. The crude and unofficial estimates of global requirements that have been made in recent years indicate that the financial burden, if properly shared, would be far from overwhelming.

So long as total project and nonproject aid for a country add up to the requirements of its economy as a whole, and repayment of foreign loans is an obligation of the economy as a whole, it will not matter greatly which projects are financed by hard loans, which by soft loans, and which by grants from abroad. The decision can be based on convenience—on the commodities the aid-giver can most readily supply, on the skills of the people it can make available for participation in the program, and (politically significant) on the character of the undertakings with which it wishes to identify itself.

The proliferation of relatively autonomous agencies from which technical and financial assistance can be secured has severely complicated the problem of coordination—of making more certain that the numerous potential sources of foreign aid (American, European, Japanese, and multilateral) actually provide the right amounts, in the right forms, at the right times. Only when the situation reaches crisis proportions have the "independent" aid-giving agencies managed to get together and offer a collective life-line to the sinking swimmer.

Although an economic crisis in India, in Spain, in Argentina, or elsewhere has to date been a necessary forerunner of real coordination of foreign aid efforts, the apparent success of the consortium approach, when it has been applied, suggests the desirability of employing the technique at an earlier stage.

Basically, the procedure is simple. Under respected leadership—that of the International Bank, for example—representatives of the major sources of foreign aid meet with officials of the country in need of aid, reappraise requirements, and agree on a division of labor for meeting those requirements. Each agency provides the type of project or other aid that it is legally authorized and administratively equipped to provide—in the amount that it has agreed to supply.

Unless some such system is institutionalized, the requirements of many of the emerging nations will not be met and, in those instances in which they are met, the burden of meeting them will be inequitably shared. The need for criteria and procedures to govern burden-sharing is as great as the need for criteria and procedures to govern the measurement of requirements.

American officials are acutely aware of these needs. In late 1960 and early 1961, the aid program was subjected to the kind of stem-to-stern review which on several previous occasions has given rise to major changes in policy. Additional fundamental changes were recommended in President Kennedy's message of March 22, 1961, to the Congress proposing "a whole new set of basic concepts and principles" to govern the foreign aid program during this "crucial decade of development." Without the support of an informed citizenry, however, desirable changes of policy will not occur—or will not survive for long if they do occur.

Selected Readings

The American Assembly, Graduate School of Business, Columbia University. *International Stability and Progress: United States Interests and Instruments.* New York: Columbia University, 1957.

Avramovic, Dragoslav, assisted by Gulhati, Ravi. *Debt Servicing Capacity and Postwar Growth in International Indebtedness.* Baltimore: Johns Hopkins Press, 1958.

———, and Gulhati, Ravi. *Debt Servicing Problems of Low-Income Countries, 1956-1958.* Baltimore: Johns Hopkins Press, 1960.

Berenson, Robert L., Bristol, William M., and Strauss, Ralph I. *Accumulation and Administration of Local Currencies: A Special Report to James H. Smith, Jr., Director, International Cooperation Administration,* August 1958. (Processed.)

Brown, William Adams, Jr., and Opie, Redvers. *American Foreign Assistance.* Washington: The Brookings Institution, 1953.

Consultants on International Finance and Economic Problems. *The Problem of Excess Accumulation of U.S.-Owned Local Currencies: Findings and Recommendations Submitted to the Under Secretary of State* [Mason Report], April 4, 1960. (Processed.)

Hoffman, Paul G. *One Hundred Countries, One and One Quarter Billion People.* Washington: Albert D. and Mary Lasker Foundation, 1960.

Millikan, Max F., and Rostow, W. W. *A Proposal, Key to an Effective Foreign Policy.* New York: Harper & Bros., 1957.

Papanek, Gustav F. *Framing a Development Program.* (International Conciliation Series No. 527.) New York: Carnegie Endowment for International Peace, 1960.

Schelling, Thomas C. *International Economics.* Boston: Allyn and Bacon, Inc., 1958. (Chaps. 26-29.)

U.N. Secretariat, Department of Economic Affairs. *Measures for the Economic Development of Under-Developed Countries: Report by a Group of Experts Appointed by the Secretary-General of the United Nations,* May 1951.

U.S. Congress, House of Representatives. *Report on Activities Carried on Under Public Law 480, 83d Congress, as Amended.* (Issued semiannually as House document.) Washington: Government Printing Office, 1955–.

U.S. Department of Commerce, Office of Business Economics. *Foreign Aid by the United States Government, 1940-1951.* (Supplement to *Survey of Current Business.*) Washington: Government Printing Office, 1952.

———, Office of Business Economics. *Foreign Grants and Credits by the United States Government.* (Issued quarterly—processed.)

U.S. Department of State. *Report to Congress on the Mutual Security Program.* (Issued semiannually—annually beginning 1960—in General Foreign Policy Series.) Washington: Government Printing Office, 1951–.

———, *The United States Economy and the Mutual Security Program.* Washington: April 1959.

———, U.S. Department of Defense, and the International Cooperation Administration. *The Mutual Security Program: A Summary Presentation.* (Annual.)

U.S. President's Committee to Study the United States Military Assistance Program [Draper Committee]. *Composite Report,* August 17, 1959. 2 vols. Washington: Government Printing Office, 1959.

Index

Africa, U.S. aid to, 37, 63, 74, 97, 99, 106

Agricultural surpluses. *See* Surplus commodity disposal.

Agricultural Trade Development and Assistance Act (Public Law 480, *1954*), 9, 10-12, 50, 52, 64, 100, 106-07, 110n, 124

Aid-financed goods, payment procedures, 14-24, 126-28

Aid-receiving countries: Debt-servicing capacity, analysis, 37-40, 44-45, 79-80, 91-105, 129-31; effects of foreign aid program on, 24-25, 34-40, 44-45, 126-28

Appropriations, for foreign aid, U.S., process, 85

Asia, 62, 122

Australia, 41

Avramovic, Dragoslav, 38n, 39n

Balance of payments: Accounting balance, 27, 28, 35, 44; defined, 26-27; effects of foreign aid on, 26-45; market balance, 27, 44; program balance, 27, 34-35, 44

Balance of payments, U.S.: Effects of foreign aid on, 28-34, 44, 122; effects of offshore procurement on, 30-33; from *1956-60* (table), 29

Balance of payments of aid-receiving countries, effects of foreign aid on, 34-40

Balance of payments of third countries, effects of foreign aid on, 40-42

Beneficiaries of foreign aid. *See* Aid-receiving countries.

Brown, William Adams, Jr., 10n, 48n

"Buy American" restrictions (*see also* Tied loans), effects, 40

Canada, 41

Capital formation in underdeveloped countries (*see also* Rate of development), 87-89, 99

Commodity Credit Corporation (CCC), 58-59

Consortium technique, 108, 112-13, 115, 118, 134-35

Cooley amendment to Public Law 480 (*1957*), 10, 11, 52, 107n, 110n, 124

Counterpart funds, 7-10, 11-12, 123, 124-25, 127-28

Country and global requirements for development aid, estimating and evaluating, 79-91, 95-96, 104-05, 113-19, 128-33

Credits. *See* Loans.

Debt-servicing capacity of aid-receiving countries, analysis, 37-40, 44-45, 79-80, 91-105, 129-31

Defense expenditures abroad, U.S., 31-32

Defense support, 8, 50, 65

Development assistance (*see also* Economic and technical aid): Consortium approach, 108, 112-13, 115, 118, 134-35; country and global requirements, estimating and evaluating, 79-81, 95-96, 104-05, 113-19, 128-29; determination between loans and grants, 91-108, 129-33; financing methods, 108-13, 120-21; program approach, 67-71, 80-89, 91, 128, 132; programming, joint, 103-04; project approach, 67-71, 80, 89-91, 92, 109-10, 128, 132; role of the foreigner, 86-87

Development Loan Fund: Commitments and disbursements, 64, 118;

139

establishment and functions, 39, 51, 67, 68, 124; procedures, 13, 14, 17, 21-22, 32, 100-01, 110-11, 125, 130
Distribution of foreign aid (see also Country and global requirements): Principles governing, 65-66; statistics, 72-77 (tables), 121-23
DLF. See Development Loan Fund.
Domar, Evsey D., 45
Draper Committee report, 57, 102n, 108n

Economic and technical aid (see also Development assistance), trends and statistics, 49, 54, 59-64, 65-66
Economic Cooperation Act (1948), 7
Eisenhower, Dwight D., directives, 32n, 33n
Employment, 86-87, 114, 132
End-users of aid-financed goods, 19-24, 92, 126
Europe (see also European Recovery Program), 47, 62, 63
European Economic Cooperation, Committee for, 85
European Recovery Program (Marshall Plan), 7, 8, 34, 48-49, 85
Expenditures for foreign aid, U.S., trends, 55-66, 72-77 (tables), 121-23
Export-Import Bank: Establishment and functions, 14, 51-52, 54; procedures, 11, 17-18, 20-21, 32, 51-52, 64, 67

Fairless Committee, 101n
Financing, determination of method, 108-13, 120-21
Foreign aid, definition, 3-6
Foreign aid program, U.S.: Administrative problems, 70-71; effects, 24, 28-34, 44-45, 126-28; major programs, 46-54; objectives, 65, 78, 108n, 118-19, 121; tabulations, 29, 72-77; volume and distribution, 55-66, 121-23
Foreign currencies. See Local currencies.
Foreign exchange earnings: Effects of

debt-servicing on, 37-38, 44, 99, 130-31; effects of surplus disposal programs on third countries, 40-42
France, 34, 63

General Agreement on Tariffs and Trade (GATT), 40-41
Germany, 34, 37, 63
Global requirements for foreign aid, evaluating, 113-19
Grant aid (see also Counterpart funds and Reverse grants): balance-of-payments effects, 28, 35, 40, 42-45; curtailment, 50, 54, 59-60; definition, 6-7, 10, 35, 55; for development needs, 10-13, 50, 107, 108, 109, 111-12, 124; for emergency needs, 9, 11-12, 107, 108; Kennedy position, 54n; loans vs. grants, 91-108, 131-33, 134; public concepts, 1, 120; surplus commodities (see Surplus commodity disposal); tied aid, 43; to India, 22-24, 106; trends, 59-66; volume, 55-56, 121-22
Great Britain, 34, 47, 63
Greece, 41, 48
Guaranties, U.S. Government, 5-6
Gulhati, Ravi, 38n, 39n

Hard loans, 14, 96-99, 127, 129-30
Haviland, H. Field, Jr., 70n, 71n
Hoffman, Paul, 94n, 117, 118n

IBRD. See International Bank for Reconstruction and Development.
ICA. See International Cooperation Administration.
IDA. See International Development Association.
India: Debt-servicing burden, 97, 99, 132; grant aid to, 22-24, 106; loans to, 20-22, 62, 64, 68-69
Inter-American Development Bank, 54, 56, 75
Interest rates on loans, 97-98, 110-11, 126
Interim Aid Program, 48
International Bank for Reconstruction

and Development: Creation and functions, 14, 47, 54; practices and projects, 18-19, 22, 38, 48, 67, 84; U.S. capital in, 56, 75

International Cooperation Administration: Administrative problems, 70-71, 125; expenditures, 33n; policies and procedures, 3, 8, 9, 13, 14, 15-17, 32, 58, 67, 70-71, 124, 128

International Development Association: functions, 39, 53-54, 130; lending activity, 69, 100; U.S. capital in, 56, 75

International Finance Corporation, 53, 56, 67, 75

International Monetary Fund, 47, 56, 75, 112

Investment Guaranty Program, 6

Kennedy, John F., policy statements, 32n, 33n, 54n, 135

Labor supply, 86-87, 114, 132

Latin America: Debt-servicing burden, 97, 99, 106, 132; U.S. aid, 62, 63, 70, 122

Legislation (*see also* Mutual security acts *and* Public Law 480), appropriations for foreign aid, process, 85

Lending agencies: International agencies, 53-54; U.S. agencies, 51-53

Letter-of-commitment procedure, 15, 17

Loans: Balance-of-payments effects, 33, 35-37, 39-40, 42-45; definition, 6-7, 35-37, 55; duration, 98; grace period, 35-36; grants vs. loans, 91-108, 129-31, 134; interest rates, 97-98, 110-11, 126; procedures of lending agencies, 14-24; public concepts, 1, 120; repayable in currency of borrower, 33, 36, 38, 50, 96, 99-105, 129-31; repayable in currency of lender, 14, 33, 96-99, 127, 129-30; tied loans, 32, 43; trends, 59-66; volume, 55-56, 121-22

Local currencies (*see also* Counterpart funds): Problems, 13, 101-03, 107, 111, 123-26, 127, 131; Public Law 480 local currency, 10-12, 124; repayments, 13-14; Section 402 currencies, 12-13

Machlup, Fritz, 27, 34

Maintenance-of-value clauses, 13-14, 92n, 126

Marshall Plan, 7, 8, 34, 48-49, 85

Mason, Edward S., 102n, 108n, 111n, 125n, 126n

Military aid program: Evaluating military equipment, 56-58; materiel assistance program, 52-53; offshore procurement, 30-31, 33; recipients, 49, 62, 63; trends, 54, 61, 78

Millikan, Max F., 116n

Mutual Defense Assistance Act (*1949*), 49

Mutual security acts, provisions, 7-8, 12-13, 49, 50, 51, 110n

Mutual Weapons Development Program, 52

NATO, 49, 65

Nonproject aid, 67-71, 128

Objectives of foreign aid program, 65, 78, 108n, 118-19, 121

Offshore procurement, 30-33, 40

Ohly, John H., 57

Opie, Redvers, 10n, 48n

Pakistan, 40-41, 41n, 64

Papanek, Gustav F., 79, 80n, 91n

Payment procedures for aid-financed goods, 14-24, 126-28

Philippine Rehabilitation Act (*1946*), 47

Point Four Program, 49

Post-UNRRA Relief Program, 48

Postwar reconstruction, 7, 8, 34, 46-49, 63, 65, 85

Private enterprise: Effects of development planning on, 81, 84; loans under Cooley amendment, 10, 11, 52, 107n, 110n, 124; relation to public lending, 5-6

Program approach, 67-71, 80-89, 91, 128, 132
Project approach, 67-71, 80, 89-91, 92, 109-10, 128, 132
Public Law 480 (Agricultural Trade Development and Assistance Act, 1954), 9, 10-12, 50, 52, 64, 100, 106-07, 110n, 124
Public Law 480 local currency, definition and uses (see also Public Law 480), 10-12, 124

Rate of development of underdeveloped countries, 69, 79-80, 86, 87-88, 92, 93-96, 99, 105, 113-14, 128-29, 131-32
Reimbursement procedure, 17
Requirements for development aid, estimating and evaluating, 79-91, 95-96, 104-05, 113-19, 128-33
Reverse grants, 10, 35, 55
Rostow, W. W., 88, 116n

Salant, Walter S., 45n, 94n
Schelling, Thomas C., 25n, 83n, 114n
Section 402 currencies, defined, 12-13
Soft loans, 13, 36, 54, 96, 99-105, 127, 129-31
Special assistance, 50-51
Surplus commodity disposal: Effect on third countries, 40-42; evaluation of commodities, 56-59; grants and sales of, 7-13, 32, 52, 64, 100, 106-07, 110n, 123, 124; launching of program, 50

Tata Iron and Steel Company, Ltd., 22, 92n
Technical and economic aid (see also Development assistance), trends and statistics, 49, 54, 59-64, 65-66
Tied loans, 20, 32, 43
Truman Doctrine, 48
Turkey, 41, 48

Underdeveloped countries: Aid requirements, estimating and evaluating, 79-81, 104-05, 113-19; debt-servicing capacity, 37-40, 93-95; International Finance Corporation loans to, 53; military aid to, 49, 52-53; problems of, emergence, 49; program approach, 67-71, 80, 86-89, 91, 128, 132; project approach, 80, 89-91, 92, 128, 132; rate of development, 69, 79-80, 86, 87-88, 92, 93-96, 99, 105, 113-14, 128-29, 131-32
United Nations Children's Fund, 54n
United Nations Expanded Technical Assistance Programme, 53
United Nations Special Fund, 53, 54n, 67
United Nations Relief and Rehabilitation Administration (UNRRA), 7, 46-47
Upton, T. Graydon, 69
"Utilized" foreign aid, defined, 55

Volume of foreign aid: Agency data, 64; regional data, 62-64, 122; trends 59-66, 121-23

Weapons Production Program, 52
Wheat-export program, U.S., effects on third countries, 41
Work Bank. See International Bank for Reconstruction and Development.